CANYON COUNTRY
WILDFLOWERS

CANYON COUNTRY
WILDFLOWERS

A Guide to Common Wildflowers, Shrubs, and Trees

In cooperation with

CANYONLANDS
Natural History Association

Second Edition

DAMIAN FAGAN

FALCONGUIDES

GUILFORD, CONNECTICUT
HELENA, MONTANA

FALCONGUIDES®

Copyright © 1998, 2012 by Rowman & Littlefield
Previously published by Falcon Publishing Inc.

Published in cooperation with the Canyonlands Natural History Association.
ALL RIGHTS RESERVED. No part of this book may be reproduced or transmitted in any form by any means, electronic or mechanical, including photocopying and recording, or by any information storage and retrieval system, except as may be expressly permitted in writing from the publisher.

FalconGuides is an imprint of Rowman & Littlefield.
Falcon, FalconGuides, and Outfit Your Mind are registered trademarks of Rowman & Littlefield.

Photos by Damian Fagan unless otherwise noted
Illustrations by DD Dowden

Map revised by Daniel Lloyd © Rowman & Littlefield

Distributed by NATIONAL BOOK NETWORK

The Library of Congress has cataloged the previous edition as follows:
Fagan, Damian.
Canyon country wildflowers: a field guide to common wildflowers, shrubs, and trees/text and photos by Damian Fagan.
p. cm.
Includes bibliographical references (p.) and index.
ISBN 1-56044-560-2 (pbk.)
1. Wild flowers—Utah—Canyonlands National Park Region—Identification. 2. Shrubs—Utah—Canyonlands National Park Region—Identification. 3. Trees—Utah—Canyonlands National Park Region—Identification. 4. Wild flowers—Utah—Canyonlands National Park Region—Pictorial works. 5. Shrubs—Utah—Canyonlands National Park Region—Pictorial works. 6. Trees—Utah—Canyonlands National Park Region—Pictorial works. I. Title.
QK189.F34 1998
582.13'09792'59—dc21 97-31824
CIP

ISBN 978-0-7627-7013-7
Printed in the United States of America

TO MY TWO FAVORITE DESERT WILDFLOWERS—
RAVEN AND LUNA—AND TO TOM NEWCOMB,
WHO INTRODUCED ME TO THE OAKS AND PINES
OF MY YOUTH.

CONTENTS

PREFACE

It was another Friday night in Moab, Utah. Downtown was active as the restaurants, shops, motels, and bars filled with patrons. But instead of heading for the neon glow and bustle of the eateries, five of us, plus our dogs, drove up to the Sand Flats area near "the world's most scenic dump." We were on a pilgrimage of sorts; we searched for *Oenothera pallida*, the pale evening primrose. When we found one ripe with floral buds, we sat down around the plant like expectant parents and waited—and watched. Slowly, oh so slowly, a flower bud unraveled, the tight sepals giving way as the petals burst forth for the grand finale. The whole process took about twenty minutes, fast enough to see and slow enough to absorb the unfolding drama. We joked about Friday nights in Moab and what the locals do for fun.

This night gave me a greater appreciation for flowers. Having considered the amount of energy expended to produce one flower, I rarely pick flowers anymore. The event also encouraged me to "experience" these plants to a greater depth, to go beyond the nomenclature and really look at the plant in all its complexity. To get down on my knees in the soft dirt or the rough gravel and inhale the flower's fragrance. To invert binoculars for a makeshift hand lens and search the flower for pollinators and even predators such as crab spiders that lurk among the blossoms. To remember that we are nature and nature *does* matter. To put aside science and facts and a system of Latin names and just sit and watch and wait for nature to unravel itself in the simple yet elegant form of a desert wildflower.

ACKNOWLEDGMENTS

Thanks to Megan Hiller and Bill Schneider of Falcon Publishing for the opportunity to write this book, and to Jessica Haberman and Julie Marsh of Globe Pequot Press for their support during this revision. Thanks also to Gloria Brown for her encouragement. I appreciate the Canyonlands Natural History Association for its continued support as well. Thanks to Julie Schroeder, a copyeditor whose botanical knowledge made this a better book. My wife, Raven, and I spent many years learning about the plants of the Canyonlands region while we were employed by the National Park Service; her enthusiasm about plants kept me interested even when I switched to watching birds. I am indebted to Joel Tuhy of the Moab office of The Nature Conservancy, and Sonja Nicoliason, a former national park ranger, for their assistance in species identification. I would also like to thank David Williams, Tara Williams, and Linda Whitham for information, ideas, and identification of several species. The National Park Service Southeast Utah Group allowed me time in its herbarium, for which I am grateful. Thanks go to Raven Tennyson for submitting photographs and answering queries. And to my daughter Luna, special gratitude—she, at almost two, has brought me to her level of seeing plants, nose to flower. And to the flowers themselves, which have brought me hours of joy and wonderment: Long may you bloom.

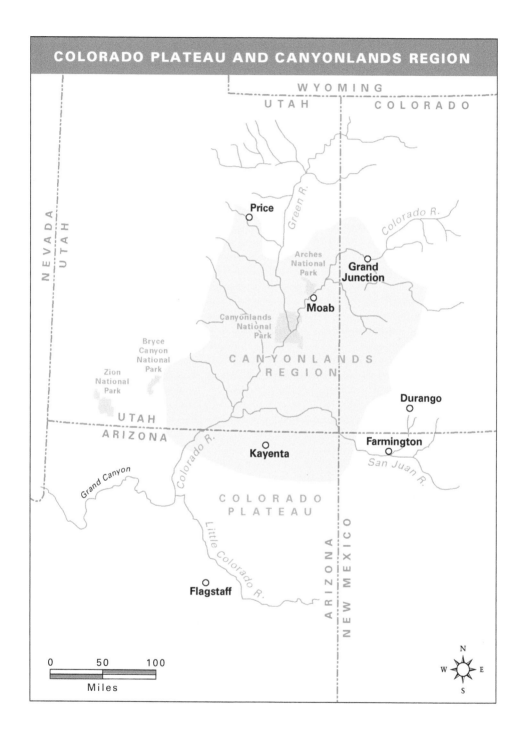

COLORADO PLATEAU AND CANYONLANDS REGION

WYOMING

UTAH | COLORADO

NEVADA | UTAH

Green R.

Colorado R.

Price

Arches
National
Park

Grand
Junction

Moab

Canyonlands
National
Park

Bryce
Canyon
National
Park

CANYONLANDS
REGION

Zion
National
Park

Durango

UTAH
ARIZONA

Colorado R.

Kayenta

Farmington

San Juan R.

Grand Canyon

COLORADO
PLATEAU

ARIZONA | NEW MEXICO

Little Colorado R.

Flagstaff

0   50   100
Miles

N
W   E
S

INTRODUCTION

The Colorado Plateau and Canyonlands Region

The Colorado Plateau is a unique geographical area that encompasses approximately 133,000 square miles and stretches over portions of Utah, Colorado, New Mexico, and Arizona. Defined by thick accumulations of sedimentary deposits, a semiarid climate, relatively high elevation, sparse vegetation, isolated mountain ranges, and vast expanses of sandstone, this landscape is world renowned for its angular topography of deep canyons, massive cliffs, and steplike escarpments.

The Canyonlands region is in the center of the Colorado Plateau; it stretches across the Four Corners area of southeastern Utah, southwestern Colorado, northeastern Arizona, and northwestern New Mexico. In this region of unparalleled geologic scenery, there are a multitude of national parks, monuments, recreation areas, state parks, wilderness study areas, and primitive areas, which showcase the colorful canyons and weird erosional features.

A continuity of sedimentary formations underlies the Canyonlands region. Comprising mudstones, siltstones, sandstones, and conglomerates, these formations greatly influence the type and composition of plants that grow in the region. Often the soil type is an erosional residue of the parent formation, which may be just a few inches below the surface. The soils, climate, elevation, and rates of evaporation together create the rigorous growing conditions that limit plant growth and species composition in the region. However, there are a large number of common plants found throughout the Canyonlands region, and these plants are the focus of this book.

Not every plant in this book is found throughout the entire region; some species have a very narrow distribution, while others grow across the Southwest. However, the plants of this field guide do represent a core of vegetation that one might see across the Canyonlands region. These plants are not restricted by political or park boundaries; they show an allegiance only to the colors of sandstone and shale.

Life Zones and Plant Communities

In the 1890s biologist C. Hart Merriam studied the vegetation and wildlife around the San Francisco Peaks near Flagstaff, Arizona, noting that there, as elsewhere in the West, were fairly distinct belts of vegetation across an elevational scale from the lowlands to

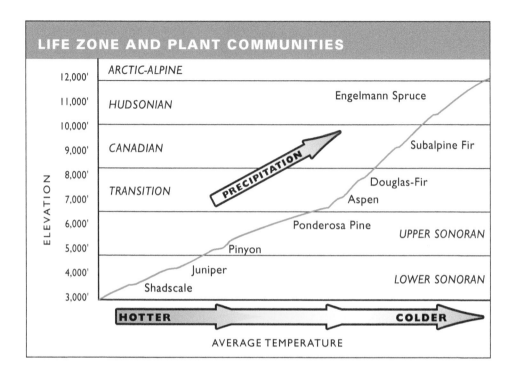

LIFE ZONE AND PLANT COMMUNITIES

the high alpine peaks. He distinguished and named these belts based on their dominant vegetation. Merriam also found relationships between certain plants and animals in these belts, or "life zones," as he called them. From lowest to highest elevation, his six life zones are Lower Sonoran, Upper Sonoran, Transition, Canadian, Hudsonian, and Arctic-Alpine. Although his life zones showed variation and tended to blend into one another, they have been a good way to broadly define the major ecological zones of the West.

Since Merriam's time, ecologists have proposed different schemes to better define the plant communities on the Colorado Plateau. Each scheme offers a varying degree of precision; however, for its general purposes, this guidebook identifies the wildflowers, shrubs, and a few trees between the lower elevational grassland/shrubland (3,800–5,000') up through the pinyon-juniper woodland (4,500–7,000'). This constitutes the upper portions of what Merriam would classify as the Lower Sonoran Zone and the Upper Sonoran Zone, and also the lower limits of the Transition Zone.

Within this elevational span one can distinguish separate smaller divisions, or *micro-habitats*, of plant communities and thus better illustrate some of the distributional ranges or habitat relationships of the plants. Characterized by the dominant woody and herbaceous

plants, but also by alkalinity, moisture, and growing substrate, these simplified communities within the 3,800–7,000' elevational range are:

1. Salt Desert Shrub. Characterized by shadscale, greasewood, and Mormon tea.
Only plant species that can tolerate highly alkaline and saline soils occupy this habitat type.

2. Lowland Riparian. Characterized by Fremont's cottonwood, water birch, boxelder, willow, tamarisk, coyote bush, rabbitbrush, and greasewood. The riparian zones
are the verdant belts of vegetation along the canyon bottoms, riverbanks, and stream-
beds. Like an oasis in the desert, this ecological community attracts many species of
birds and animals.

3. Hanging Garden. Characterized by maidenhair fern, scarlet monkeyflower, helle-
borine, and alcove columbine. As water moves downward through the porous sandstone,
it may encounter an impervious rock layer. At this point water flows horizontally until it
reaches an exposed edge of the sandstone or drips from an alcove wall. Hanging gardens
are the lush plant communities in these alcoves; the highest number of endemic plants
occurs within hanging gardens. These communities may also be present beneath the large
pour-offs in the canyon drainages, regardless of rock type.

4. Blackbrush. Communities dominated by extensive stands of blackbrush across
uniformly thin soils.

5. Sand Desert Shrub. Characterized by old man sage, yucca, Indian ricegrass, and
shinnery oak. Many of the plants in this community have extensive root systems that stabilize the sand dunes; others can "readjust" to shifting sands.

6. Mixed Desert Shrub. May include a mixture of rabbitbrush, fourwing saltbush,
blackbrush, narrowleaf mahogany, and other species. Often different soil types overlap and
intergrade in this community.

7. Cool Desert Shrub. Characterized by big sagebrush, winterfat, and rabbitbrush.
This community is based on loamy or sandy soils.

8. Pinyon-Juniper Woodland. Characterized by pinyon pine, Utah juniper, singleleaf
ash, and Utah serviceberry. This community covers a vast portion of Utah and the Canyonlands region. Plants occur on rocky soils or jointed bedrock.

9. Warm Desert Shrub. Characterized by blackbrush and old man sage. This community is based on hot, dry slopes and rocky outcrops.

10. Mountain Brush. Characterized by Gambel's oak, serviceberry, big sagebrush, and
mountain mahogany. This community covers large portions of the mountain foothills and
shaded canyons.

11. Ponderosa Pine. Characterized by ponderosa pine, manzanita, and aspen. This community is found in areas with drier soil types at higher elevations or in the upper reaches of shaded canyons.

Another term used in this guide is **weedy,** which describes plants that occur in disturbed or damaged sites nearly everywhere throughout the region. Many of these plants are not native to the Canyonlands region.

Soils and Other Environmental Conditions

Two main aspects of soils—texture and chemical composition—have direct effects on plant growth and species composition. Unless sediments are carried by wind and water a long distance, the weathering and erosion of local sedimentary rock generally create the various soil types found in an area. Erosion of the coarse-textured Navajo and Wingate sandstones results in sandy soils, while erosion of the shales and mudstones of the Mancos Shale and Morrison Formations results in fine-textured soils. Each soil's moisture-holding capacity, which is important for plant survival, decreases from deep sandy soils, through rocky loams, to shallow fine-textured clays and silts. Since plants vary in their ability to survive in dry soils, some plants are present only in particular soil types.

Generally, coarse-textured soils are dominated by woody shrubs or trees with long taproots that can penetrate deep into the soil to reach water during periods of drought. Fine-textured soils, high in clays and silts, support grasses, low-growing perennials, and annual plants whose shallow-growing root systems can absorb available moisture in the surface and near-surface soil layers, especially right after a rain. Soils of intermediate texture support a mix of these two contrasting forms.

The soil's chemical composition, which is related to its texture, also influences the species of plants that grow in a location. For instance, soils high in sodium and alkalinity, such as those derived from the Mancos Shale Formation, inhibit plant growth and thus affect species composition. In this way some species of plants are narrowly restricted to certain geologic strata and the soil conditions created by the erosion of the strata. One example is the Canyonlands biscuitroot, *Lomatium latilobum*, which occurs along rock fins of the Entrada and Navajo sandstones in a few locations within the region.

Other environmental factors that affect plant distribution and species composition are elevation and aspect. With increases in elevation, temperature decreases and precipitation increases. Along this temperature/moisture gradient, the lowland plant communities, including semidesert grasslands and shrublands, give way to the pinyon-juniper woodlands and then to other forests at higher elevations. But elevation may be compensated for by aspect: North-facing slopes are generally cooler than south-facing slopes. Cool, moist alcove sites may contain plants usually found in the higher elevations, such as Douglas-fir trees (*Pseudotsuga menziesii*).

Annual precipitation, rates of evaporation, maximum summer temperatures, and the vegetation present are some other factors that define landscapes. Due to these characteristics, the Canyonlands region is a "cold desert"—a semiarid region, with a tendency toward cold winters and hot, dry summers. The average high and low temperatures are 41°/21°F for the winter and 90°/60°F for the summer.

This elevational range receives an average of 9 inches of precipitation annually. Seasonal precipitation typically includes gentle, steady rains in winter and spring and brief but deluging cloudbursts in late summer. Snowfall varies considerably from year to year, with the greatest average amounts falling in January, April, and November. It is not uncommon in April to have snow one week and 60°F temperatures the next.

Table 1. Climate information from Canyonlands National Park

	J	F	M	A	M	J	J	A	S	O	N	D
Temperature (in °F)												
Extreme High	67	75	85	91	101	109	111	108	108	94	80	68
Extreme Low	28	-21	7	16	23	32	38	36	28	-6	-8	-15
Average High	39	46	55	64	73	87	92	90	82	68	51	38
Average Low	19	23	30	34	46	58	62	60	51	40	29	22
Precipitation												
Rain (in inches)	.63	.29	1.07	.76	.71	.50	1.15	.92	.69	1.0	.86	.60
Snow (in inches)	5.5	1.2	2.8	3.4	0.2	–	–	–	–	0.5	3.3	2.4
Thunderstorms	0	1	1	4	4	9	11	5	2	0	0	0

Environmental Considerations

Endemic Plants

Primarily due to the unique geologic history and climate of the Colorado Plateau, there is a high level of plant endemism—plants restricted to a geographic region, topographical unit, or soil condition—in the Canyonlands region. Roughly 55 percent of the endemic plants on the Colorado Plateau occur on sand and gravel soils, and about 25 percent occur on clays,

Cryptobiotic crust

Cryptobiotic crust

shales, or muds. Because of their limited distribution, a few are federally listed as endangered or threatened species protected under the Endangered Species Act.

Cryptobiotic Crust

Cryptobiotic crusts are found throughout the world, but they are especially important on the Colorado Plateau. These crusts are dark brown to black in color, lumpy, and highly contoured, looking much like a miniature cityscape. When young or poorly developed, they may be nearly invisible to the naked eye. Cryptobiotic crusts are important soil stabilizers in this sandy environment and aid plants in obtaining moisture and nutrients, especially nitrogen, from the soil.

Mosses, soil fungi, lichens, and green algae occur in these soils, but cyanobacteria make up the bulk of the crust and can make up 95 percent of the crust's biomass. The microscopic cyanobacteria secrete a thick, extracellular, gelatinous sheath that surrounds and coats their cells and the filaments they form. Soil particles adhere to this sticky sheath, making larger, more complex clumps that provide cohesion and strength to the soil. When moistened, filaments of the cyanobacteria partially extrude from the main sheath. These filaments produce new sheaths around themselves and leave the abandoned sheath material behind; there is more abandoned than inhabited sheath material in a well-developed crust.

Cryptobiotic crusts are very fragile and often protect the entire thin topsoil layer. Crushing the crusts severely inhibits their normal functions and may result in removal of the material and the topsoil via erosion. Rates of recovery vary depending on the severity of the impact, precipitation, source material, and other factors, but some disturbed crusts may take more than fifty years to recover.

When hiking in the desert, avoid these soil crusts by staying on established trails or walking in sandy washes or on slickrock areas. Backtrack if necessary or look for game trails to follow to keep from crushing the soil crusts.

Plant Adaptations and Characteristics

Plants in the Canyonlands

There are many environmental conditions that plants must contend with in this desert environment: hot, dry summers; cold winters; strong, drying winds; long periods between rainfall; herbivory; intense solar radiation; and other rigorous growing conditions. Plants, unlike wildlife, are literally rooted in place and cannot relocate when drought or herbivores threaten. Plants have nevertheless adapted various physical or metabolic characteristics that enable them to live and thrive here.

In the Canyonlands region total plant cover is not 100 percent, so plants rarely compete with each other for available light the way plants might in other environments. Instead a plant's success depends more on temperature, water, and available nutrients. During winter most plants are dormant or have greatly reduced growth rates; precipitation in winter and early spring recharges the soil moisture content. Springtime, before temperatures become too high or soil moisture too low, presents the optimal window for maximum photosynthetic rates for many plants.

The leaf is the main site where photosynthesis takes place. Water vapor, oxygen, and carbon dioxide move from within the leaf into the air, and vice versa, through lens-shaped openings called stomata. Located mainly on the underside of the leaf, away from direct sunlight, the stomata open and close with the demands of photosynthesis, while minimizing water loss to the desert air. Available sunlight for photosynthesis is not a problem for desert plants; losing excessive amounts of water during photosynthesis can be a problem.

To reduce this potential problem, desert plants share many physical and metabolic traits that help to conserve moisture. Small leaf size; various hairs or projections on the surface to reduce the drying effect of the wind; thick, waxy leaf surfaces; deep taproots or barely subsurface extensive lateral root systems; succulent stems (cacti); and evergreen or deciduous leaves are just a few ways plants have adapted to the desert environment.

Both leaf strategies—evergreen and deciduous—benefit desert plants. Evergreen leaves remain on the plant throughout the year and are shed gradually so that the plant is never barren. This low energy expenditure for leaf production allows the plant to use that energy elsewhere. Deciduous plants lose their leaves at the end of the growing season as the plant enters a dormant period over the winter. By dropping the leaves, the plant does not need to expend energy on leaf maintenance during the nongrowing months.

Not all plants put on their maximum growth in the spring, however. Certain species, like rabbitbrush (*Chrysothamnus* sp.), have deep taproots and can continue photosynthetic activity throughout the summer drought period. Other species, like cliffrose (*Purshia mexicana*), correlate plant growth and flowering with the onset of summer rains and can enter a second growth and flower phase in years with heavy August and September rainfall.

A combination of physical and metabolic characteristics help plants grow in salty or saline soils. The weathering of certain formations, particularly the Mancos Shale and Chinle Formations, results in high concentrations of salts in the upper levels of the soils, often in the root zone. Only certain plants can tolerate these highly alkaline soils that ordinarily would inhibit the growth of most plants. Salt-tolerant plants have evolved different ways of surviving in a saline environment. Winterfat *(Krascheninnikovia lanata)* blocks the uptake of excessive salts at the roots. Saltbush (*Atriplex canescens*) has specialized structures on the leaf surface into which excessive salts are placed; these structures eventually rupture, excreting the salts to the outside. Other plants may deposit salts back to the soil via an internal return system. Adaptations to the desert environment have resulted in a variety of fascinating forms and interesting lifestyles, enabling plants to exist in this seemingly harsh landscape.

Energy from the Sun

Photosynthesis is the metabolic process by which plants use carbon dioxide from the atmosphere, solar energy, and chlorophyll to produce organic molecules—carbohydrates—necessary for plant growth. Another way of describing photosynthesis is that it is the conversion of light energy to chemical energy. Carbohydrates and simple sugars then are turned into more complex substances by enzyme activity. There are three pathways of photosynthesis, each distinguished by the first chemical reaction that happens upon the capture of carbon dioxide. All plants use one of these methods, and the efficiency of each varies with different temperatures and the amount of water available. Cacti use the CAM (Crassulacean Acid Metabolism) pathway, which allows the plant to open its stomata (porthole-like openings) at night to capture carbon dioxide and store it in a cell chamber for use in the daylight. The plant completes the process of photosynthesis in the daylight. By opening the stomata at night, when temperatures are cooler, the plant reduces the amount of water it loses to the atmosphere.

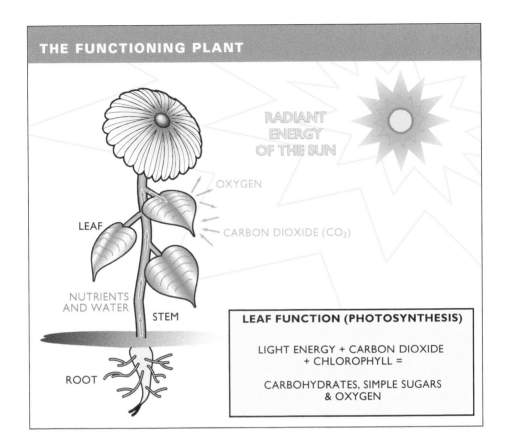

THE FUNCTIONING PLANT

RADIANT ENERGY OF THE SUN

OXYGEN

CARBON DIOXIDE (CO_2)

LEAF

NUTRIENTS AND WATER

STEM

ROOT

LEAF FUNCTION (PHOTOSYNTHESIS)

LIGHT ENERGY + CARBON DIOXIDE
+ CHLOROPHYLL =

CARBOHYDRATES, SIMPLE SUGARS
& OXYGEN

The Functioning Plant

The diagram above shows the general functions of a plant. Roots absorb water and minerals from the soil so that they can be transported to the higher parts of the plant. The stem has conduits for transporting water and minerals to the leaves and for taking products made in the leaves—carbohydrates, proteins, lipids, etc.—to other parts of the plant. Leaves contain chlorophyll and other pigments necessary for photosynthesis. The sugars and others products of photosynthesis and the raw materials taken from the soil are either used immediately or stored by the plant.

Pollination

Flowers contain the structures necessary to complete pollination. *Pollination* is the transfer of male spores, or *pollen*, from the *anther* at the end of the *stamen* to the *stigma*, which is the tip of the female part of the flower, the *pistil*. When pollen grains reach the stigma, they germinate, much like a seed, and a *pollen tube*, or tubes, grows downward into the *style*, the stalk of the pistil. In these tubes the male sex cells, or *gametes,* form. For most of the flowering plants (the angiosperms) in this book, the pollen tube grows through the tissues of the pistil. (The only gymnosperms in this book are the two-needle pinyon, Utah juniper, ponderosa pine, Douglas fir, and Mormon tea.) The pistil nourishes the tube as it grows, and when the pollen tube is near the female gamete in the *ovule*, the male gametes release and fertilization takes place. The transfer of pollen to the stigma of a flower is one of the greatest technical achievements of the plant kingdom; the logistics of this have helped create the fascinating variety of flowers seen today.

The fossil record is a stone testament to the innovation of the plant kingdom over millions of years; it reveals spore-producing ferns, primitive fernlike trees that bore seeds (not spores), cone-bearing plants (conifers), and the more modern orchids with their specialized methods of pollination. Throughout this history there was a noted change from wind pollination to animal pollination, a conclusion based on the structure of fossilized flowers, which occurred at about the same time pollinating insects became numerous.

Generally there are three main ways ovules become fertilized: wind pollination, animal pollination (including insects, birds, and mammals), and self-pollination, which occurs in only a small percentage of plants. Wind pollination is considered the more "primitive" form of pollination; the gymnosperms and about 15 percent of the angiosperms, such as grasses and many trees, are wind pollinated. Wind pollination is a chancy method, used primarily by plants that grow in close proximity to one another or where there are few insects to do the job. To increase the odds of pollination, many wind-pollinated plants release tremendous amounts of pollen into the wind from their usually smaller and less-showy flowers. Some have separate male and female flowers, often arranged in dense clusters, to further this strategy. Some species release their huge amounts of pollen before their leaves develop, to increase the odds of contact even more.

The evolution of animal pollination, which benefits both pollinator and plant, created a tremendous amount of variation in flower structure, since no single floral type perfectly suits all types of potential pollinators. About 85 percent of all flowering plants are insect pollinated. Differences in flower size, shape, coloration, and arrangement are shown in the simplified chart of Table 2. This does not cover all the groups of insects, and one may observe many different types of insects on one flower.

Most insects move pollen from flower to flower more reliably than the wind. Some insects are generalists and visit different types of plants, not selecting just one type of flower during their foraging. Bees, on the other hand, are more "faithful" as pollinators;

they select one or a few species of plants and regularly visit only those flowers, which count on the bees for pollination and reward them with nectar and pollen.

Plants tend to consistently attract certain insect pollinators, and those pollinators evolve to select the flowers that fulfill their needs as well. Nectar, a sugary bribe or reward, attracts the pollinators. Certain plants may time their nectar release to coincide with the times of pack foraging activity of certain insects or birds, and thus do not spend precious energy providing nectar to nonpollinating species. For example, members of the penstemon genus (*Penstemon*) and the paintbrush genus (*Castilleja*) produce nectar twice a day to coincide with the feeding periods of their pollinators. Nectar production at midday is conservative for members of the paintbrush genus that are hummingbird pollinated, due to the lowered activity period for the birds around midday.

Table 2. Simplified chart showing some relationships between flowers and pollinator groups. (Adapted from Howe and Westley 1988)

Pollinator	Flower Color	Flower Depth	Odor
Beetles	Usually dull	Flat, bowl-shaped	Strong
Flies	Variable	Moderately deep	Variable
Bees	Blue, white, pink, but not pure red	Flat or broad tube	Usually sweet
Wasps	Dull or brown	Flat or broad tube	Usually sweet
Hawkmoths	White or pale green	Deep, narrow, tubular	Strong, sweet
Small moths	White or green (nocturnal); red, purple, pink (diurnal)	Moderately deep	Moderately sweet
Butterflies	Bright red, yellow, blue	Deep, narrow, tubular	Moderately strong, sweet
Birds	Bright red	Deep, with wide spur or tubular	None

One classic example of a pollination relationship is between the *pronuba,* or yucca moth (family Megathymidae), and the yucca (*Yucca* sp.) plant. After mating, the female moth collects some sticky pollen grains and pollinates a flower. At the same time, she deposits her eggs in the flower's ovary. The developing larvae feed on some of the forming seeds as they mature; thus this tightly connected insect-plant relationship benefits both partners.

Visual acuity for insects is less than that for humans, and their ability to distinguish shape and form from a distance is relatively poor. Many flowers have developed special patterns of color, called *nectar guides*, which function as landing lights, attracting these pollinators and orienting them to the nectar. Most yellow and white flowers are highly reflective of light and are visited by a large variety of insects, but blue flowers are frequented more by bees than by any other insect group.

Several plants also change their floral color after pollination. The flowers of dwarf evening primrose (*Oenothera caespitosa*) fade to a pinkish color; likewise, the central spot on several of the lupines (*Lupinus* sp.) fade from white to yellowish. Such color changes indicate that pollination has taken place and tell insects to search for other flowers to pollinate.

Plant Characteristics

This section will help to define some of the terms and physical characteristics of the plants in this book. Technical terms are kept to a minimum; for their definitions see the **Glossary.**

Many desert plants are **perennials,** plants with more or less woody stems and deep or long roots that last at least three years. Two types of perennials exist: **woody** shrubs and trees, and **herbaceous** perennials that die back to underground roots or stems each winter. **Biennials** have a two-year life cycle. The plant becomes established during the first season, often producing a basal rosette of leaves. During the second season, the plant flowers, produces seed, and then dies. **Annuals** complete their life cycle in one growing season, their future housed in dormant seeds. Annuals require specific amounts of winter and spring moisture before the seed germinates; chemical inhibitors within the seed prevent premature germination. In drought conditions the seeds do not germinate and remain dormant, possibly for many years.

Sometimes it is difficult to distinguish perennials from annuals. To identify perennials, look for woody stems; underground structures for food storage such as tubers, bulbs, and corms; or dried flowering stems and leaves from previous years.

Leaf Structure
Important features to note about the leaves and stems are:
• Arrangement of the leaves along the stem: Are they opposite, alternate, or whorled?
• Simple versus compound leaves: if compound, how many leaflets?
• Leaf margin: entire, toothed, wavy, or lobed?
• Are the leaves only basal, or are they also found along the stem?
• Does the leaf have a stalk (petiole)?
• Are there hairs or other projections along the stem or on the leaf surfaces?

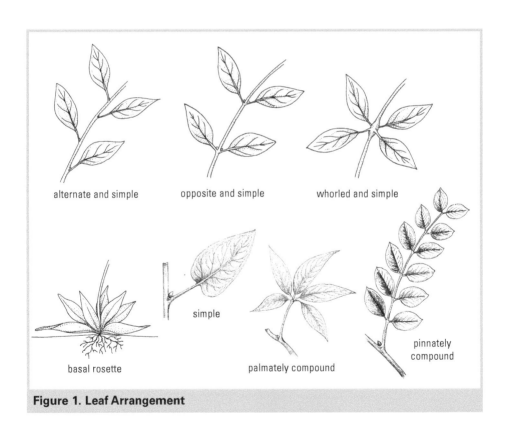

Figure 1. Leaf Arrangement

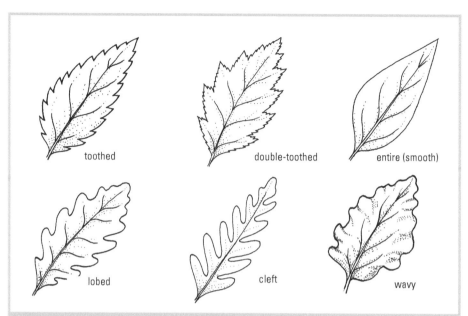

Figure 2. Leaf Margin

toothed

double-toothed

entire (smooth)

lobed

cleft

wavy

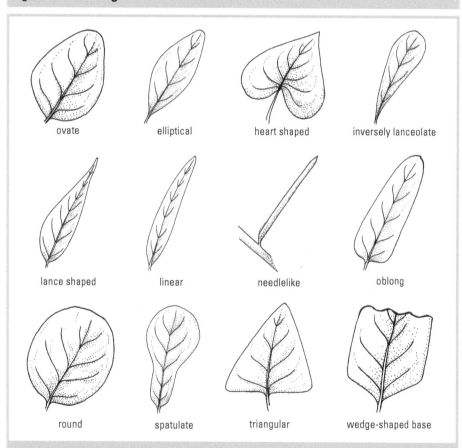

Figure 3. Leaf Shapes

ovate

elliptical

heart shaped

inversely lanceolate

lance shaped

linear

needlelike

oblong

round

spatulate

triangular

wedge-shaped base

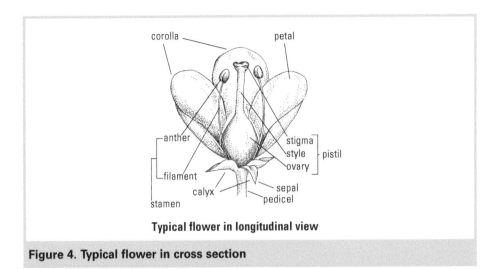

Typical flower in longitudinal view

Figure 4. Typical flower in cross section

Flower Structure

The diagram in Figure 4 shows a generalized flower in cross section. The variation and number of flower parts are key characters for identification. The **sepals,** or outer series of parts, surround the base of the flower. Sepals are often green and inconspicuous, but they may be colorful and showy as in the paintbrushes (*Castilleja*). Together they are called the **calyx,** which may be composed of separate or fused sepals.

Inside the calyx of most flowers are the **petals,** an inner series of generally colorful parts. Petals also vary in size and shape and may be separate or fused. The petals are collectively called the **corolla;** some plants, however, may lack a corolla, or the sepals and petals may be identical. Together, the calyx and corolla function to attract pollinators and protect the sex organs at the center of the flower.

Inside the flower are the **stamens**, the pollen-producing structures. Typically long and thin, the stamens have a clublike or elongated appendage at the tip—the **anther**—from which pollen is released. Stamens may number from none to more than one hundred per flower.

The **pistil,** or seed-producing structure, has three main parts: stigma, style, and ovary. Pollen reaches the **stigma** or pollen receptor, which sits atop the stalklike **style.** The style connects the **ovary** and the stigma and is the tubelike structure that the pollen tube grows through to reach the ovary. Within the ovary are the **ovules,** the structures that become the seeds after fertilization.

Here again, variation is the theme song. For example, some flowers lack a style; ovules may vary in arrangement and number, which determines the type of seed or fruit that develops. Many flowers have both male (staminate) and female (pistillate) parts within one flower, but some plants have separate male and female flowers on the same plant and some have either male or female parts on separate plants. The term **monoecious** ("one home") is used to describe a species where male and female flowers are on one plant; **dioecious** ("two homes") refers to unisexual flowers being found on separate individual plants.

Two families with unique flower types are shown in Figures 5 and 6. These flowers are in the sunflower (Asteraceae) and pea (Fabaceae) families.

Members of the sunflower family (Asteraceae) have an elaborate flower arrangement (see Figure 7). A **flower head,** which looks like one flower, is actually a dense cluster of a few to several hundred tiny flowers. The flower head has a series of **bracts,** more or less modified leaves that surround the base of the flower head. The calyx of each of the tiny flowers is absent or reduced to bristles, scales, or hairs that form a crown at the top of the seed known as the **pappus;** this is often a key in identifying the species. Members of the Asteraceae family produce two types of flowers—**ray flowers** and **disk flowers**—and may possess either one type of these flowers or both. See Figure 5 for generalized flowers of this family. A straplike limb forms the corolla of the ray flower and is usually brightly colored. The disk flower has a small, tubular corolla, usually with five lobes but with no rays.

Members of the pea family (Fabaceae) have a calyx that surrounds five modified petals. The upper petal, or **standard,** is erect, spreading, and usually the longest of the five. The two side petals, or **wings,** closely surround the **keel,** which are the two fused lower petals. See Figure 6 for a typical flower of the Fabaceae.

Classifying and Naming Plants

Carl Linnaeus (1707–1778) was a Swedish naturalist who developed the modern system of binomial nomenclature, in which every living thing has a genus and species name. Linnaeus created a descriptive system that standardized the terminology and naming of plants and animals, as well as how to systematically organize the information. The system provides a common language for all to use. For instance, the binomial name *Mimulus eastwoodiae* (scarlet monkeyflower) consists of a Latin or Greek generic (referring to genus) name followed by a specific epithet (referring to species). Linnaeus based his work on that done by various individuals all the way back to Aristotle; his work *Species Plantarum* (1753), for

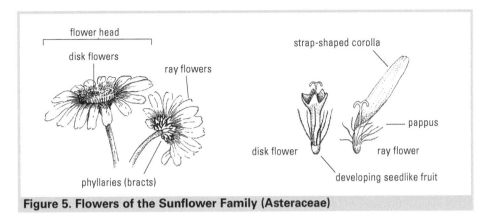

Figure 5. Flowers of the Sunflower Family (Asteraceae)

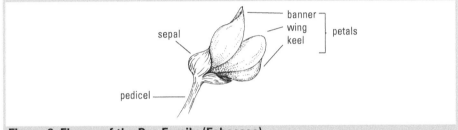

Figure 6. Flower of the Pea Family (Fabaceae)

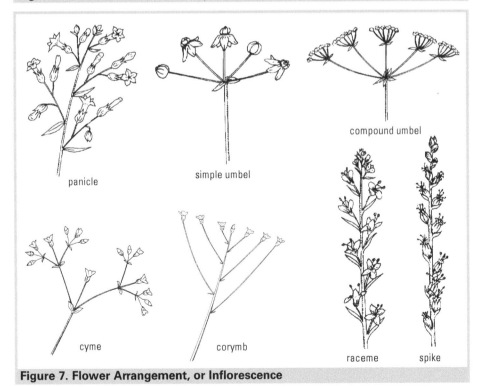

Figure 7. Flower Arrangement, or Inflorescence

plants, and the tenth edition of his *Systema Naturae* (1758), for animals, form the foundations for scientific naming still in use today.

For plants, Linnaeus based his system, known as the sexual system, on the number, union, or length of stamens and the structure of the ovary. Because such features do not necessarily show evolutionary relatedness, this has been called an artificial system. His system greatly clarified and simplified the identification and description of known and newly discovered taxa.

Within Linnaeus's nomenclatural hierarchy, plants with similar sexual features were lumped together in families, then sorted out into different genera—finer divisions of the family group. The genera were then split into the various species. From the family level upward to the level of kingdom, the groupings all have distinct endings. For all the family names, such as Asteraceae or Liliaceae, the ending is -*aceae*. Many of the scientific names provide clues as to features of the plant and/or its native range; its discoverer may also honor someone by giving the plant that person's name.

A Utah Flora by Stanley L. Welsh, N. Duane Atwood, Sherel Goodrich, and Larry C. Higgins is the primary botanical key for plants in Utah. All of the scientific names (except for a few family names) used in this field guide are from that text. Common names, which may vary, also follow those used in *A Utah Flora*, with a few exceptions.

USING THIS GUIDE

This field guide covers 230 species of plants found in the Canyonlands region. Plants are separated into groups based on flower color and then arranged alphabetically by family (Agavaceae, Apiaceae, etc.) and then by genus and species within the family. Scientific names are standardized, whereas common names are not, so the plants are not arranged alphabetically by common names.

To identify a flower, turn to the corresponding color section and search among those pages for the plant. Several plants are bicolored or may exhibit a range of colors because of genetic variation. If the plant does not appear within the primary color section, turn to the secondary color section and search there. Please note that a few of the photos in the book show fruits instead of flowers. For some species, the fruits better define the plant or are visible longer during the growing season than the flowers.

Each plant has a brief **Description** section to provide identifying information, including characteristics such as the size, shape, form, and color of stems, leaves, flowers, and fruits. A hand lens is helpful in viewing minute structures such as hairs, bracts, flower parts, and seeds. See the illustrations in the Plant Characteristics section and the definitions in the Glossary to help with descriptive terminology.

The **Bloom Time** section provides a general time frame that a species blooms. Of course, this varies due to seasonal weather conditions and elevation.

The Habitat/Range section provides the general habitats and distribution for each species.

The **Comments** section provides natural history information about the plant and often explains the derivation of the scientific name. If a plant is endemic to the Canyonlands region or is threatened or endangered, it is noted here. The comments also describe notable uses of a plant, including medicinal properties and edibility. Readers interested in historical or modern herbalism, homeopathy, or flower essences should check the Reference section in the back of the book.

Some comparisons to similar species are noted; however, to include each of the more than 1,000 species of plants found in the area would result in a much larger guide. If at times you are only able to determine the genus or family level of a plant, take heart; occasionally, even trained botanists are stumped.

This section includes white, cream, and gray flowers and those that grade into whitish shades of pink or blue.

DATIL YUCCA
Yucca baccata
Agave family (Agavaceae)

Description: Perennial. Dense basal cluster of stout, straplike leaves that are 12–40" long and 1–2" wide. Short stems are single or clumped together. Fibers along leaf margins curl. Flowering stalks may barely rise above leaves; bell-shaped flowers are 1½–3¼" long and white to cream in color. Fruits are large and fleshy at maturity.

Bloom Time: April to June.

Habitat/Range: Pinyon-juniper to ponderosa pine and riparian plant communities, 4,750–6,660', in the Southwest.

Comments: Ancestral Puebloans made cordage, mats, sandals, baskets, and cloth from the leaf fibers; they ate the flowering stalks, flowers, and fruits; and they made soap from the roots. *Baccata* (fruited) refers to the large pods.

HARRIMAN'S YUCCA
Yucca harrimaniae
Agave family (Agavaceae)

Description: Perennial, solitary or clumped plant. Rigid leaves are lance-shaped, pale green, sharp-pointed at the tips, and 4–20" long. With age, white fibers curl along leaf margins. Flower stalk rises above leaves 14–30" or more. Greenish-yellow to cream flowers are bell-shaped, 1½–2" long, and tinged with purple. Fruit is a cylindrical capsule with a short beak.

Bloom Time: April to June.

Habitat/Range: Warm desert shrub up to mountain brush communities in the Southwest.

Comments: Native Americans plaited the tough plant fibers to make cordage. Flower buds, flowers, and tender flower stalks are edible. Narrow-leaf yucca (*Y. angustissima*) is similar but has flatter, linear leaves, a white or pale green style, and longer flowering stems and flower clusters.

POISON IVY

Toxicodendron rydbergii
Cashew family (Anacardiaceae)

Description: Perennial. Woody shrub to 3', or sparsely branched single stems in a loose cluster. Compound leaves are long-petioled with 3 (rarely 4 or 5) toothed or lobed, dark lusterless green leaflets, 1–4½" long. Tiny, whitish male and female flowers are densely arranged in leaf axils on separate plants. Cream to yellow berries may remain over winter.

Bloom Time: March to June.

Habitat/Range: Riparian and moist locations across the West.

Comments: *Toxicodendron* (toxic plant) refers to the nonvolatile oil, urushiol, on the leaves and stems, which may cause uncomfortable skin irritation. *Rydbergii* is for the botanist Per Axel Rydberg (1860–1931).

BASIN WHITE-CUP SPRING-PARSLEY

Cymopterus purpurascens
Carrot family (Apiaceae)

Description: Low-growing perennial plant, 2–7" tall, that rises from a tuberous root. Smooth, compound leaves are 2–3 times pinnately divided, with 3–6 pairs of oppositely arranged leaflets. Flowering stalks are 1½–5" long, arise in groups of 1–3, and bear clusters of flowers with white to purplish petals that have a greenish or purplish midvein. Fruit is a winged seed.

Bloom Time: February to May.

Habitat/Range: Desert shrub, grasslands, sandy sites.

Comments: *Cymopterus* (wavy wing) refers to the wavy margins or wings of the individual seeds. *Purpurascens* (becoming purple) indicates the changing color of the flowers.

TOMENTOSE AMSONIA
Amsonia tomentosa
Dogbane family (Apocynaceae)

Description: Perennial, 8–24" tall, forming dense clusters of leaves and flowering stems. Leaves alternate, smooth or densely hairy; lower ones are lance-shaped and larger than upper threadlike leaves. Bluish-white flowers, borne in terminal clusters, have slender tube-shaped corollas, ⅜–¾" long. Flowers flare at top. Several-seeded pods contain brownish, cylindrical seeds.

Bloom Time: April to June.

Habitat/Range: Desert shrub communities up to 5,000' in the Southwest.

Comments: *Amsonia* is for Dr. Charles Amson, an eighteenth-century Virginia physician. *Tomentosa* refers to the wool-like covering created by the many small and matted hairs.

SPREADING DOGBANE
Apocynum androsaemifolium
Dogbane family (Apocynaceae)

Description: Perennial, low growing or with stems up to 2' tall. Opposite leaves are lance- to egg-shaped and often droop from stem. Cut stems exude milky sap. Small, ¼"-long urn-shaped flowers are borne in clusters; flowers are white to pinkish. Fruit is a slender pod up to 3" long that hangs downward.

Bloom Time: June to August.

Habitat/Range: Sagebrush to aspen communities from British Columbia to Arizona.

Comments: *Androsaemifolium* (*Androsaemum*-like leaves) indicates the similarity of the spreading dogbane leaves to those of another plant, *Androsaemum*. Native Americans used the strong stem fibers to make cordage. Another common name is flytrap dogbane—insects become trapped in the V-shaped openings at the base of the pistil.

COMMON DOGBANE
Apocynum cannabinum
Dogbane family (Apocynaceae)

Description: Perennial. Thin reddish stems with milky latex arise in spindly clusters to 3'. Stems and leaves branch oppositely or in a whorled pattern. Variably sized leaves are lance- or egg-shaped in outline, smooth above and downy beneath; lower leaves may be stemless. White flowers, ⅛" wide, cup-shaped, and borne in clusters at top or along short side-stems. Long, thin pods hang down at maturity.

Bloom Time: May to August.

Habitat/Range: Disturbed sites and fields in riparian or streamside communities. Widespread in the United States.

Comments: Another common name is Indian hemp; *cannabinum* (like hemp) refers to the strong cordage that was made by plaiting the stem's long fibers. Cymarin, a chemical in the roots, was used as a cardiac medicine and was listed until 1952 in the *United States Pharmacopoeia*.

BROADLEAF MILKWEED
Asclepias latifolia
Milkweed family (Asclepiadaceae)

Description: Perennial that grows up to 3' tall on stout stems. Broad, rounded leaves are 2–8" long and borne on short stems. Stems and leaves exude milky sap when cut or broken. Flower clusters are borne in leaf axils along upper stem on short flowering stalks. Star-shaped individual flowers are greenish-white, ½–¾" long, with stout column and curved horns. Fruit is a smooth seedpod, 3–4" long.

Bloom Time: April to July.

Habitat/Range: Disturbed sites in mixed desert shrub to juniper and hanging garden communities from southeastern Utah to Texas and California.

Comments: *Latifolia* (with broad leaves) refers to the large, broad leaves. The leaves are hairy when young and become smoother with age.

WHORLED MILKWEED
Asclepias subverticillata
Milkweed family (Asclepiadaceae)

Description: Perennial plant to 4' high, usually with slender, unbranched stems. Threadlike leaves, up to 3" long, arise in opposite pairs or whorls of 3–5 leaves. Small-stalked flower clusters, with up to 20 flowers per cluster, are found in upper portion of plant. Each white, star-shaped flower is less than ½" long, with 5 white petals and 5 erect, white hoods. Slim seedpods rise upward and are 2–4" long.

Bloom Time: May to July.

Habitat/Range: Disturbed sites or roadsides in blackbrush to mountain brush communities in the Southwest.

Comments: Between the hoods on each flower are slits that can trap the leg(s) of a visiting insect. As the insect pulls its leg free, "saddlebag" structures of pollen attach to the leg. The insect then carries these to the next flower, which is thus cross-pollinated by the previous one. Whorled milkweed is poisonous.

YARROW

Achillea millefolium
Sunflower family (Asteraceae)

Description: Aromatic perennial with flowering stalks up to several feet tall. Fernlike basal leaves are pinnately divided; lower leaves are stalked, but smaller upper leaves lack a stalk. Flat-topped clusters of small white flowers contain mostly disk flowers (10–30) and few ray flowers (3–5). Tiny black seeds lack any appendages.

Bloom Time: April to October.

Habitat/Range: Sagebrush to high elevation communities in the Four Corners region. Widely distributed in North America.

Comments: *Achillea* is named for the Greek mythological hero Achilles. *Millefolium* (1,000-leaved) refers to the finely divided leaf segments. In medieval times yarrow was used as a poultice to stop bloody wounds; another common name is soldier's woundwort.

ROSY PUSSYTOES

Antennaria microphylla
Sunflower family (Asteraceae)

Description: Mat-forming perennial that bears horizontal runners and upright flowering stems, 2–19" tall. Hairy basal leaves are paddle- or lance-shaped; stem leaves are smaller. Clusters of white to pinkish flower heads are made up of only disk flowers. Fruit is a tiny seed with white hairs.

Bloom Time: April to September.

Habitat/Range: Sagebrush to alpine communities throughout the West.

Comments: *Antennaria* (a ship's yard) is from the derivation for an insect's antenna; the white hairs on the seed resemble butterfly antennae. *Microphylla* (small-leaved) indicates the size of the leaves. The common name evokes the flower's resemblance to a cat's furry toe.

EMORY SEEPWILLOW
Baccharis salicina
Sunflower family (Asteraceae)

Description: Shrub 3–12' tall, many-branched, often striped. Leaves are ⅜–3½" long, linear or spatula-shaped, and irregularly toothed or along entire margins. Female and male flowers in loose conical or pyramid-like clusters are at upper ends of stems and on separate plants. Female flowers have several series of sticky bracts; seeds have fine, ½"-long white hairs.

Bloom Time: May to September.

Habitat/Range: Riparian or hanging garden communities, 2,500–4,500', in the Southwest to Mexico and southern California.

Comments: *Baccharis* is in honor of the Greek god of wine, Bacchus, due to the sweet aroma of the root. Seepwillow describes the plant's willow-like leaves and habit of growing in wet places. The former name of the species was *B. emoryi,* in honor of William H. Emory (1811–1887), an American soldier and lieutenant of topographical engineers in 1838.

STEVIA DUSTY-MAIDEN
Chaenactis stevioides
Sunflower family (Asteraceae)

Description: Annual, 1½–14" tall, that's very hairy throughout. Leaves, up to 4" long, are linear, grayish-woolly, and lobed or cleft usually halfway to middle; individual lobes may be smaller. Flower heads, 1 inch wide, are solitary or clustered and arise on short stems. Stamens often protrude above white disk flowers; some outer flowers may be enlarged and raylike.

Bloom Time: April to July.

Habitat/Range: Mixed desert shrub to pinyon-juniper communities, often in sandy soils.

Comments: *Chaenactis* is from the Greek *chaino* (to gape) and *actis* (ray), referring to the enlarged, irregular, raylike outer disk flowers of many species. *Stevioides* (like *Stevia*) refers to this species' resemblance to plants of another genus. *C. douglasii*, or Douglas' dusty-maiden, is a related species also found in the Southwest.

ROSE-HEATH
Chaetopappa ericoides
Sunflower family (Asteraceae)

Description: Perennial, up to 6" tall, may grow in loose clusters. Stems have small, stiff hairs. Leaves, up to ⅛" long, are linear or spatula-shaped and taper to a point. Flower heads are solitary or in clusters; bracts that subtend flowers are in 3–5 series. Each whitish flower has 12–25 rays, about ¼" long, surrounding circle of yellow disk flowers. Seeds have hairs lying close to surface.

Bloom Time: May to August.

Habitat/Range: Salt desert shrub to ponderosa pine communities in the Southwest and east to Kansas.

Comments: *Chaetopappa* (bristly pappus) refers to the hairs on the seeds. *Ericoides* (heathlike) refers to the overall small size and leaf pattern of the plant.

GRAY THISTLE
Cirsium undulatum
Sunflower family (Asteraceae)

Description: Perennial that grows 2–5' tall and has stems covered with dense white hairs. Leaves form basal rosette; leaves are 2–10" long and deeply divided or lobed. Lobes are toothed or lobed with spines along margins. Leaves along stem are smaller. Rounded flower heads, 1½–2½" wide, are creamy white or pink and contain only disk flowers. Bracts below heads are brown, lance-shaped, and with spiny tips spreading.

Bloom Time: May to July.

Habitat/Range: Blackbrush to pinyon-juniper communities in disturbed sites in the Southwest.

Comments: *Cirsium* is from the Greek name *kirsion* (swollen vein) because one species of thistle was used to treat swollen veins. *C. neomexicana*, the Utah thistle, is similar, but the flower heads are more cylindrical and the involucre is greenish and long-spined.

HORSEWEED
Conyza canadensis
Sunflower family (Asteraceae)

Description: Annual, up to 40" tall, with smooth or slightly hairy stems that branch in the upper portion. Leaves are ¾–3⅛" long, linear to inversely lance-shaped; margins have fine hairs. Numerous flower heads are urn-shaped and ⅛–¼" tall; minute ray flowers are white or purplish and surround about 20 yellow disk flowers.

Bloom Time: April to September.

Habitat/Range: Disturbed sites, mostly riparian, across North America.

Comments: *Conyza* is the Greek name for the plant, and *canadensis* (of Canada) refers to the plant's distribution. This weedy species occurs throughout North America and Europe.

SPREADING DAISY
Erigeron divergens
Sunflower family (Asteraceae)

Description: Annual, biennial, or short-lived perennial, 2–20" tall. Stems have soft, spreading hairs. Basal leaves are inversely lance- or spatula-shaped, ⅜–2½" long, narrow, and covered with hairs. Leaves along stem are similar but smaller. Flower heads may be numerous per plant, with 75–150 blue, pink, or white rays, about 1" wide, surrounding yellow disk flowers.

Bloom Time: April to July.

Habitat/Range: Wide range of habitats and elevations from riparian to aspen communities, 3,000–9,050', in the West.

Comments: *Erigeron* is from Greek *eri* (early) and *geron* (old man), because the plants flower early in the season and the seed's bristles resemble an old man's gray hair. Thomas Nuttall first collected this plant in the 1830s in the Rocky Mountains.

VERNAL DAISY
Erigeron pumilis
Sunflower family (Asteraceae)

Description: Perennial to 20" tall; lower branches are clothed with ashy to brown withered leaves. Basal leaves are linear or inversely lance-shaped, ¼–3½" long, and covered with coarse, stiff hairs. Stem leaves are smaller or absent. Few to numerous flower heads, ¼–½" wide, with 50–100 white or pink rays surrounding a cluster of yellow disk flowers. Bracts below flower heads may have long, soft hairs.

Bloom Time: April to June.

Habitat/Range: Salt desert shrub, mountain brush, pinyon-juniper, and ponderosa pine communities from Idaho to New Mexico.

Comments: *Pumilis* (dwarf) refers to the small stature of this hairy plant.

TIDYTIPS
Layia glandulosa
Sunflower family (Asteraceae)

Description: Annual plant that grows 4–12" tall. Basal leaves are lobed or toothed, covered with stiff glandular hairs, and ½–3" long. Flowering heads have a cluster of yellow disk flowers surrounded by numerous 3-lobed white ray flowers. Flower heads are 1–3" wide. Fruit is a seed that bears whitish hairs.

Bloom Time: April to June.

Habitat/Range: Grasslands and pinyon-juniper communities from British Columbia to Baja California and east to Arizona.

Comments: *Layia* honors George Tradescant Lay (c. 1800–1845), an English botanist who collected plants while on the Beechey Voyage (1825–1828) that visited Asia, Hawaii, Alaska, California, and South America. *Glandulosa* (glandular) refers to the sticky hairs that cover the plant.

SILVERY TOWNSENDIA
Townsendia incana
Sunflower family (Asteraceae)

Description: Short-lived perennial, ¾–4" tall, that has stems conspicuously covered with white hairs. Spatula- to inversely lance-shaped leaves are ¼–1½" long and hairy. Flower heads on short stalks are solitary or few, ½–1" wide, and with 13–34 rays that are white on the upper surface and pink to lavender below.

Bloom Time: April to June.

Habitat/Range: Blackbrush, mixed desert shrub, and pinyon-juniper communities from Wyoming to New Mexico.

Comments: *Townsendia* honors David Townsend (1787–1858), an amateur botanist from West Chester, Pennsylvania. *Incana* (hoary) refers to the white, hairy stems.

FPO-please
scan slide

YELLOW-EYE CRYPTANTH
Cryptantha flavoculata
Borage family (Boraginaceae)

Description: Low-growing perennial, 4–16" tall, with 1 to several slender, hairy stems. Leaves are linear to spatula-shaped, 1–4" long, and covered with short, stiff hairs. Corolla is a short white tube with spreading lobes and a yellow throat. Fruit is 4 nutlets, each with a rough surface.

Bloom Time: March to June.

Habitat/Range: Sagebrush, pinyon-juniper, mountain brush, and ponderosa pine communities, 4,650–6,700', in the Southwest.

Comments: Many members of the *Cryptantha* genus are identified by the minute variations on the seed's surface as well as by other features. *Flavoculata* (a little yellow) refers to the flower color. Some botanists refer to this as *Oreocarya flavoculata.*

SLENDER CRYPTANTH
Cryptantha tenuis
Borage family (Boraginaceae)

Description: Low-growing perennial, 4–9" tall, with 1 to several stems arising from a basal cluster of leaves. Stem and leaves have stiff, short hairs. Leaves are linear to spatula-shaped, mostly basal, and ¾–2¾" long. Flowers are ¼–⅜" long; white corolla tube flares to funnel-shaped at tip, just longer than calyx.

Bloom Time: April to May.

Habitat/Range: Salt desert shrub to pinyon-juniper communities in southeastern Utah.

Comments: Cryptanth is endemic to the Colorado Plateau. A related plant, the long-flowered cryptanth *(C. longiflora),* has flowers that extend far beyond the calyx tip.

BINDWEED HELIOTROPE
Heliotropium convolvulaceum
Borage family (Boraginaceae)

Description: Annual, low-growing or with elongated, sprawling branches up to 20" long. Lance- to egg-shaped leaves are ½–1" long and pointed at tips. White funnel-shaped flowers are borne along stem in leaf axils and have 5-lobed corollas with yellowish centers. Flowers are ½–1" wide. Mature fruits often break apart into 4 single-seeded nutlets.

Bloom Time: April to September.

Habitat/Range: Sandy soils in blackbrush to sagebrush communities up to 5,270'.

Comments: The sweet-smelling flowers open in the evening and attract moths as pollinators. *Heliotropium* (sun turning) refers to the blooming time of this genus during the summer solstice. *Convolvulaceum* (like *Convolvulus*) refers to this plant's similarity to field bindweed *(C. arvensis).*

WOODY TIQUILIA
Tiquilia latior
Borage family (Boraginaceae)

Description: Perennial, forming low-growing, dense mats 8–24" in diameter. Leaves are linear or elliptical, ⅜" long, with stiff hairs along margins. Funnel-shaped flowers, ⅛" wide, are whitish pink and borne among leaves. Fruits are clumped into 4 single-seeded nutlets.

Bloom Time: April to July.

Habitat/Range: Salt desert shrub and pinyon-juniper communities up to 6,550' in Utah, Arizona, and Nevada.

Comments: The flowers of this Colorado Plateau endemic open in the afternoon. *Tiquilia* is a name given to this plant by South American natives, and *latior* (wide) refers to the growth habit of the plant.

SPECTACLE-POD
Dithyrea wislizenii
Mustard family (Brassicaceae)

Description: Annual, with several to many erect stems to 20" tall. Basal leaves are gray, wavy-toothed, or irregularly lobed, 1–3" long, and covered with minute hairs. Leaves along flowering stalk are smaller. Flowers are white to greenish, ⅜–¾" wide, arising in ladder-like fashion; top flowers are in a rounded cluster. Rounded seedpods, ½" long, are fused together along a common midline.

Bloom Time: April to June.

Habitat/Range: Sandy soils and dunes in mixed desert shrub to ponderosa pine communities in the Southwest.

Comments: *Dithyrea* (two shields) describes the seedpods, which resemble a pair of eyeglasses. *Wislizenii* honors Friedrich Adolph Wislizenus (1810–1889), a German physician, traveler, and author, who immigrated to the United States in 1835, joined a trading caravan to Mexico in 1846, and made many observations of the local flora and fauna.

WEDGELEAF DRABA
Draba cuneifolia
Mustard family (Brassicaceae)

Description: Annual, 5" tall, with basal rosette of wedge-shaped leaves covered with stiff hairs. White flowers, ¼" long, have 4 spatula-shaped petals and arise on short stalks congested at top of main flowering stalk. Seedpods are flat, more or less elliptical, and contain 20 or more tiny seeds.

Bloom Time: April to June.

Habitat/Range: Warm desert shrublands to ponderosa pine communities across the West.

Comments: *Draba* is the Greek name for a related plant, and *cuneifolia* (wedge-shaped leaf) describes the leaves. This tiny plant may grow in dense profusion, but is easily overlooked.

MOUNTAIN PEPPERPLANT
Lepidium montanum
Mustard family (Brassicaceae)

Description: Perennial (or, less commonly, biennial) that grows up to 4' tall; a highly variable species. Leaves are basal only or basal and along stem, variously shaped, and ¼–5" long. Basal leaves may be cleft to midline or entire; stem leaves are narrow and entire along margin. White flowers, 4-petaled and up to ⅛" across, are arranged in tight clusters. Seedpods are ⅛" long, wide, and egg-shaped.

Bloom Time: April to July.

Habitat/Range: Variety of mixed desert shrub, pinyon-juniper woodlands, and shrub communities at higher elevations in the Southwest.

Comments: Seedpods are edible and peppery. The form of the plant is high variable. *Lepidium* is from the Greek *lepis* (scale), a reference to the flattened shape of the seedpods. *Montanum* (of the mountains) refers to the elevational range of this plant. This plant was first collected by Thomas Nuttall around 1835. Moab peppergrass *(Lepidium moabense)* is a Colorado Plateau endemic found in southeastern Utah in hanging gardens and seeps.

LITTLE TWISTFLOWER
Streptanthella longirostris
Mustard family (Brassicaceae)

Description: Wiry annual up to 2' tall. Bluish-green leaves are lance-shaped or elliptical in outline; leaf edges are toothed and wavy or smooth. Flowering stalk has few small leaves and 2-toned urn-shaped flowers; greenish or purplish sepals contrast with white or purplish-veined petals. Long, narrow, pointed seedpods hang downward.

Bloom Time: March to June.

Habitat/Range: Sandy or gravelly soils in warm desert shrub to pinyon-juniper communities.

Comments: *Streptanthella* is the diminutive of *Streptanthus*, from the Greek *streptos* (twisted) and *anthos* (flower), referring to the twisted petals of the flower. *Longirostris* (long beak) refers to the seedpod's pointed tip.

HEART-LEAF TWISTFLOWER
Streptanthus cordatus
Mustard family (Brassicaceae)

Description: Perennial with smooth stems, 1–3' tall. Basal leaves are spatula-shaped with toothed margins, bluish-green, and with heart-shaped bases that clasp stems. Flowers have 4 purple sepals that pinch inward at top, almost obscuring 4 purple to chestnut petals. Flattened pods are 2–3" long and curve upward.

Bloom Time: March to June.

Habitat/Range: Mixed shrublands to mountain brush communities from Oregon to New Mexico.

Comments: *Streptanthus* (twisted flower) refers to the form of the flowers, and *cordatus* (heart-like) refers to the heart-shaped base of the upper stem leaves.

ELEGANT THELYPODY
Thelypodiopsis elegans
Mustard family (Brassicaceae)

Description: Biennial or short-lived perennial, 5–38" tall, with smooth stems (but may be densely hairy below). Basal leaves are ⅜–2½" long with margins entire or irregularly toothed; upper leaves are smaller and linear to lance-shaped. Flowers are small, 4-petaled, arising on short stems from main flowering stalk, and pink to lavender or white with purplish veins. Narrow seedpods are 1½–2¼" long and curve upward.

Bloom Time: March to June.

Habitat/Range: Salt desert shrub to mountain brush communities in fine to coarse soils from southeastern Utah to southwestern Wyoming.

Comments: *Elegans* (elegant) refers to the tall, graceful stature of the plant. Tall thelypody *(Thelypodium integrifolium)* also occurs in the region.

SIMPSON'S FOOTCACTUS
Pediocactus simpsonii
Cactus family (Cactaceae)

Description: Solitary or colonial rounded stems grow 1–7" high and 1½–10" wide. Stems are covered with tubercles (swollen areas) that bear brown to blackish central spines and white radial spines. Flowers are ½–1½" wide; petal-like parts range from white to greenish, yellowish, or pinkish. Fleshy fruit is green and may turn reddish with age.

Bloom Time: May to July.

Habitat/Range: Mixed desert shrub to ponderosa pine communities, up to 8,850', from Washington to New Mexico.

Comments: *Pediocactus* is from the Greek *pedio* (plains), referring to the growing locations of this cactus. *Simpsonii* honors James H. Simpson (1813–1883), a topographical engineer who first collected this cactus in Nevada.

FENDLER'S SANDWORT
Arenaria fendleri
Pink family (Caryophyllaceae)

Description: Perennial, low-growing and forming cushions or mats. Clustered basal leaves are ⅛–2" long, straight, and pungent-smelling. Two to six pairs of leaves present along flowering stem. Flowers in loose clusters, each ¼–½" wide, with 4 or 5 greenish sepals washed with purple and 4 or 5 creamy yellow to white petals. Fruit is a small capsule with 6 teeth.

Bloom Time: April to July.

Habitat/Range: Sagebrush to higher elevation communities in the Southwest.

Comments: *Arenaria* is from the Latin *arena* (sand), a reference to the growing location of these plants. *Fendleri* is for Augustus Fendler, a German immigrant who collected many Southwestern plants for Asa Gray, the famous Harvard botanist.

WINTERFAT
Krascheninnikovia lanata
Goosefoot family (Chenopodiaceae)

Description: Compact shrub, mostly 3' or taller. Leaves and branchlets are covered with dense long hairs. Linear or lance-shaped leaves, ⅜–1½" long. Flower clusters are borne in leaf axils toward branch tips. Male and female flowers are separate but on same plant; 2–4 male flowers per axil and female flowers in dense clusters. Fruits are covered with long white hairs.

Bloom Time: April to August.

Habitat/Range: Salt desert shrub, cold desert shrub, grasslands, and pinyon-juniper communities up to 8,860', from the Yukon to the Southwest.

Comments: Winterfat is an important winter browse plant for wildlife and livestock. *Krascheninnikovia* honors Stephan Krascheninnikov (1713–55), a Russian botanist. *Lanata* (wool-like) refers to the hairy branches, leaves, and fruits.

GREENLEAF MANZANITA
Arctostaphylos patula
Heath family (Ericaceae)

Description: Often a low-growing, sprawling shrub with gnarled stems and smooth, reddish-brown bark. Leaves alternate egg-shaped to elliptical, ¾–2" long, and yellow-green. Pink to white bell-shaped flowers are borne in loose, hanging clusters. Fruit is a white, green, or brown berry.

Bloom Time: April to July.

Habitat/Range: Ponderosa pine communities, 4,275–9,320' in Oregon south to Arizona.

Comments: *Arctostaphylos* is from the Greek *arktos* (bear) and *staphule* (bunch of grapes), in reference to the clustered fruit that is edible but tart.

FENDLER'S EUPHORB
Chamaesyce fendleri
Spurge family (Euphorbiaceae)

Description: Low-growing perennial with reddish-purple stems, 2–8" long. Sap is a milky latex. Oval to lance-shaped leaves are opposite and ¼–⅜" long. Tiny flower clusters resemble a single flower, but separate male and female flowers are arranged in clusters. Below flower cluster are two separate petal-like appendages. Cluster has 15–35 male flowers to 1 female flower.

Bloom Time: April to September.

Habitat/Range: Blackbrush, salt desert, mixed desert shrub, and pinyon-juniper communities up to 7,240' in the Southwest and northward to South Dakota.

Comments: *Chamaesyce* (creeping fig) refers to the sprawling nature of Fendler's euphorb. The milky sap of this plant can be applied to burns or insect bites for treatment, but most euphorbs are toxic. *Fendleri* is in honor of the botanist Augustus Fendler (1813–1883), who collected plants in the Southwest. Formerly called *Euphorbia fendleri; Euphorbia* is in honor of Euphorbus, the Greek physician of King Juba of Numidia, a Roman province in North Africa.

STINKING MILKVETCH
Astragalus praelongus
Pea family (Fabaceae)

Description: Perennial, 4–36" tall, stems erect and often forming clumps. Compound leaves, 1–9" long, have 7–33 elliptical or lance- to inversely lance-shaped leaflets. Leaflets are slightly hairy below. Flower stalks are 1½–12" tall with 10–33 tightly clustered flowers. Greenish calyx contrasts with cream-colored corolla, which is ½–1" long and often is tipped with purple. Broadly elliptical seedpods are upright or curve downward.

Bloom Time: April to June.

Habitat/Range: Clay or silty soils, often selenium-rich, in salt desert shrub and pinyon-juniper communities in the Southwest.

Comments: Fleshy seedpods become woody with age and may remain attached to withered stems over the winter. Grows in selenium-bearing soils. Plants may exude the unpleasant odor of selenium; hence the common name. *Prae* (before) and *longus* (long) may refer to the dense flower cluster spreading out as the plant matures.

WESTERN PRAIRIE-CLOVER
Dalea oligophylla
Pea family (Fabaceae)

Description: Perennial with smooth, clustered stems, 16–36" tall. Compound leaves, ½–2" long, alternate with dark, dotlike glands and are composed of 4–9 elliptical leaflets that are often folded in half. Tiny white flowers have 4 narrow, petal-like segments fused with the tube formed by stalks of 5 stamens. Flowers are densely clustered at tops of smooth stalks.

Bloom Time: April to August.

Habitat/Range: Sandy sites or rock crevices in mixed desert shrub, pinyon-juniper, and hanging garden communities from Canada to Mexico and east to Iowa.

Comments: The crushed leaves are lemon-scented. *Dalea* honors Samuel Dale (1659–1739), a British botanist. *Oligophylla* (few flowered) refers to the minimal number of leaves on the plant. Western priairie-clover was previously placed in the genus *Petalostemon;* the name is in reference to how the stamens are fused to the petals.

WILD LICORICE
Glycyrrhiza lepidota
Pea family (Fabaceae)

Description: Perennial, 1–4' tall. Compound leaves, 3–6½" long, have 13–19 lance-shaped leaflets. Leaflets are pointed at tips, smooth above, and glandular dotted or slightly hairy below. Flowers are arranged along elongated axis with 20–50 flowers per axis. Bell-shaped calyx is less than ⅜" long; corolla is white to cream and ⅜–½" long. Pods, ⅜–¾" long, are covered with hooked spines.

Bloom Time: April to July.

Habitat/Range: Moist sites in riparian and pinyon-juniper communities throughout most of the United States, except the Southeast.

Comments: *Glycyrrhiza* is from the Greek *glykos* (sweet) and *rhiza* (root), referring to the sweet flavor of the roasted roots, which were eaten by Native Americans. *Lepidota* (scaly) refers to the brown scales on the leaves. European licorice (*G. glabra*) is commercially used in cough syrups, laxatives, and confections. The hooked pods catch on animal fur, which helps to disperse the seeds.

FENDLERBUSH

Fendlera rupicola
Hydrangea family (Hydrangeaceae)

Description: Many-branched shrub, 3–6' tall; bark of twigs is reddish, turning gray with age, and longitudinally ridged and grooved. Opposite leaves are linear or elliptical, ⅜–1⅛" long, with sparse soft hairs and prominent midrib. White flowers are solitary or 2–3 together at ends of short branches; 4 petals are narrow at base and ⅜–1⅛" long. Fruit is a woody capsule, often persistent on the plant.

Bloom Time: April to July.

Habitat/Range: Sagebrush, pinyon-juniper, and ponderosa pine communities up to 8,650' in Utah, Colorado, and Arizona to California.

Comments: This striking plant blooms on talus slopes along the Colorado River near Moab, Utah. *Fendlera* is for Augustus Wilhelm Fendler (1813–1883), botanical explorer and collector in the American Southwest. *Rupicola* (growing on rocks) describes the plant's habit of growing in rocky areas. Native Americans used the hard wood of the shrub for digging tools and arrow foreshafts.

COMMON HOREHOUND

Marrubium vulgare
Mint family (Laminaceae)

Description: Weedy perennial that grows 8–40" tall, with square-shaped stems densely covered with hairs. Leaves are opposite, hairy, oval, with rounded or pointed tips, deeply veined, and toothed along margin. Dense cluster of tiny white flowers blooms in leaf axils. Corolla is 2-lipped; upper lip is erect, and 3-cleft lower lip spreads.

Bloom Time: May to July.

Habitat/Range: Disturbed sites throughout North America. Native to Eurasia.

Comments: *Vulgare* (common) refers to the wide distribution of this Eurasian native, and *hore* (hairy) refers to the hairs on the leaves and stems. Extracts have been used in syrups for coughs or lung ailments.

FUNNEL LILY
Androstephium breviflorum
Lily family (Liliaceae)

Description: Low-growing perennial from 1"-wide buried bulb. Often found growing alone, these lilies may bloom in profusion during some years. Grasslike leaves may be curved or straight, with 1–3 per plant. Leafless flowering stalk bears small cluster of 3–8 dirty green or white ¾"-wide flowers with purple markings. Capsule is 3-lobed and ½" long.

Bloom Time: March to May.

Habitat/Range: Fine-textured soils in blackbrush to pinyon-juniper communities from Nevada to Colorado.

Comments: *Androstephium* is from the Greek words *ardrus* (man) and *stephium* (crown) and indicates the round feature of the flower. *Breviflorum* (short flowers) refers to the flower length.

SEGO LILY
Calochortus nuttallii
Lily family (Liliaceae)

Description: Perennial that grows from onion-like bulb. Stems, 3–18" tall, usually have 3 long, linear, grasslike leaves. Striking flowers, 1–1½" wide, have 3 narrow sepals that are greenish to purplish outside and pale inside; may grow in clusters of 1–3 flowers. Three large white, cream, or lavender petals have pointed tips and a hairy gland located in a patch of yellow on inside base of petal. Gland is often bordered above by a purplish crescent. Fruit is a pointed capsule.

Bloom Time: April to July.

Habitat/Range: Grasslands, sagebrush, pinyon-juniper, and up to aspen communities throughout the Intermountain West.

Comments: State flower of Utah; the bulbs are edible. *Calochortus* (beautiful grass) refers to the long leaves. *Nuttallii* is for the naturalist and Harvard professor Thomas Nuttall (1786–1859), who wrote the *Genera of North American Plants* in 1818. Some years these plants bloom in profusion and cover large patches of desert.

STAR-LILY
Leucocrinum montanum
Lily family (Liliaceae)

Description: Low-growing perennial up to 5" tall from deeply buried roots. Narrow linear leaves are 2–10" long. Fragrant white flowers are borne on short stalks, 2–5" long, that may barely rise above ground. Showy flowers are often arranged in clusters; individual flowers are 1–2" wide. Fruit is an egg-shaped capsule.

Bloom Time: April to June.

Habitat/Range: Sagebrush up to ponderosa pine communities, often in sandy soils, from Oregon to New Mexico.

Comments: *Leucocrinum* is from the Greek *leukos* (white) and crinon (lily). *Montanum* (of the mountains) refers to the higher elevation occurrence of this plant. Star-lily may remain dormant for many years, and then bloom when conditions are suitable.

STAR-FLOWERED FALSE SOLOMON'S SEAL
Smilacina stellata
Lily family (Liliaceae)

Description: Perennial with upright or arched stems, 10–30" tall. Broad lance-shaped leaves are 2½–8" long. Five to 10 white, starlike flowers are borne in a terminal cluster. Sepals are long and straplike. Fruit is a mottled berry that turns red with age.

Bloom Time: April to August.

Habitat/Range: Hanging gardens and moist sites in pinyon-juniper up to spruce fir communities across much of North America.

Comments: *Stellata* (starlike) refers to the shape of the flowers. Though the berries are edible, they are of poor quality. *S. racemosa*, false Solomon's seal, has very broad leaves and a dense spike of white flowers. *Maianthemum stellata* is the synonym.

PANICLED DEATH CAMAS
Zigadenus paniculatus
Lily family (Liliaceae)

Description: Perennial from a bulb; slender stems reach 35" tall. Straplike basal leaves are ½" wide and up to 18" long. Flower heads are arranged in loose cluster with youngest ones at top of flowering stalk. Individual flowers are white, ¼" wide, and made up of 6 sepals. Fruit is a capsule.

Bloom Time: April to June.

Habitat/Range: Blackbrush, grasslands, warm desert shrub up to ponderosa pine communities across much of the arid West.

Comments: *Paniculatus* (flowers in a panicle) describes the arrangement of the flowers. Death camas contains toxic alkaloids; hence the common name.

WATSON'S DEATH CAMAS

Zigadenus venenosus
Lily family (Liliaceae)

Description: Perennial, grows 7–35" high from a bulb. Leaves are mostly basal, 5–17" long, and straplike, narrowing at tips. Flowers are borne in a cluster. Individual flowers have white or cream segments and are about ¼–½" long. Fruit is a capsule that splits open at maturity.

Bloom Time: April to July.

Habitat/Range: Moist areas that dry out, such as meadows and streamsides, in sagebrush, pinyon-juniper, and higher plant communities to 9,320', from British Columbia to Mexico and across the West.

Comments: The bulbs are poisonous; hence the common name. *Zigadenus* (paired glands) and *venenous* (venon) describe the potency of the plant. Another *Zigadenus*, alcove death camas *(Z. vaginatus)*, occurs in hanging gardens and seeps in the Southwest.

SAND VERBENA

Abronia fragrans
Four O'Clock family (Nyctaginaceae)

Description: Perennial, with stems 7–32" tall, smooth or covered with glandular hairs. Leaves are opposite; leaf blades are lance- to egg-shaped or linear, ⅜–3½" long, and covered with fine sticky hairs. White flowers are borne in dense clusters of 25–80 flowers. Flowers have tube-shaped corolla, ⅜–1" long, with lobed and wavy flare at end, and open primarily in the evening. Fruit is a winged seed.

Bloom Time: March to June.

Habitat/Range: Sandy soils in blackbrush, sagebrush, and ponderosa pine communities from Montana to Mexico.

Comments: *Fragrans* (fragrant) refers to the sweet-smelling flowers that bloom at night. *Abronia* is from the Greek *abros* (delicate), referring to the flowers. Sand grains adhere to the sticky hairs on the leaves. The winged seeds are blown across dunes as a means of dispersal.

NARROWLEAF UMBRELLAWORT
Mirabilis linearis
Four O'Clock family (Nyctaginaceae)

Description: Clump-forming perennial with upright, smooth stems, 8–40" high. Leaves are linear, ¾–4" long, and sparingly toothed. Generally 3 flowers arise from group of fused bracts; flowers are whitish or pink, ½" wide, the tube short and flaring, and petal-like segments unequal in length.

Bloom Time: May to September.

Habitat/Range: Wide variety of habitats, 3,500–8,470', from Montana to Mexico.

Comments: *Linearis* (linear) refers to the narrow leaves. One variety has pink or purplish flowers.

WILLOW GAURA
Gaura parviflora
Evening Primrose family (Onagraceae)

Description: Lanky annual or biennial, to 5' tall; stems are covered with glandular hairs. Elliptical to lance-shaped leaves are ¾–4" long; upper ones are smaller. Numerous, delicate whitish-pink flowers, ⅛–¼" long, are borne along elongated stem at top of plant. Fruits are rectangular, up to ⅜" long, and contain 3–4 seeds.

Bloom Time: April to September.

Habitat/Range: Moist sites in riparian communities from Washington to the Southwest and east to Louisiana.

Comments: *Gaura* is from *gauros* (proud), in reference to the erect flowers. *Parviflora* (small flowered) refers to the flower size. The long, thin flower stalk may curl like a lizard's tail; another common name is lizardtail.

DWARF EVENING PRIMROSE
Oenothera caespitosa
Evening Primrose family (Onagraceae)

Description: Low-growing perennial, with leaves forming basal rosette. Leaves, ½–8" long, are long-stemmed, and leaf blade is toothed, lobed, entire, or deeply cleft to the middle. White flowers are 2–3½" wide; tube is 1–5" long and 4 petals are lobed. Yellow stamens and style extend far above flower's throat. Fruit is a woody, rough-textured capsule.

Bloom Time: March to August.

Habitat/Range: Wide variety of habitats throughout the Four Corners region.

Comments: *Oenothera* (wine-scented) refers to the use of the roots in winemaking. *Caespitosa* (low-growing) describes the stature of the plant. Flowers open in late afternoon and evening. Pollinated by nocturnal insects, the flowers turn pink after pollination. There are several varieties of this plant.

PALE EVENING PRIMROSE
Oenothera pallida
Evening Primrose family (Onagraceae)

Description: Perennial with reddish stems, 4–28" long, growing erect or low. Lance-shaped to elliptical leaves, ⅜–3½" long, have various margins—toothed, lobed, entire, or deeply cleft. Solitary white flowers, about 1½" wide, grow from leaf axils. Flowers have 4 petals with yellow patches at base. Fruit is a woody capsule.

Bloom Time: March to August.

Habitat/Range: Grasslands and variety of shrublands up to ponderosa pine communities across the West.

Comments: Flowers turn pink or lavender after pollination. *Pallida* (pale) refers to the petal color. Flowers open in the late afternoon or evening and last about 1 day.

SAN RAFAEL PRICKLY-POPPY
Argemone corymbosa
Poppy family (Papaveraceae)

Description: Moderately branched perennial, 8–36" tall, with stout, spiny stems. Leaves are inversely lance-shaped, 1–6" long, armed with stout spines below (sparingly above) and lobed halfway to middle of leaf. White flowers, 1½–2½" wide, have numerous yellow stamens; outer petals are as broad as they are long, and inner ones are much broader than long. Capsule is football-shaped and spiny.

Bloom Time: May to August.

Habitat/Range: Sandy desert shrub communities in the Southwest.

Comments: *Argemone* is from the Greek *argema* (cataract), a disorder of the eye that this plant was used to treat. It was also used as a purgative in substitution for syrup of ipecac. *Cormybosa* refers to the arrangement of the flat-topped clusters or corymbs of flowers. Plants are toxic.

INDIAN-WHEAT
Plantago patagonica
Plantain family (Plantaginaceae)

Description: Low-growing annual plant covered with dense woolly hairs. Leaves, ⅜–8" long, are linear or narrow and inversely lance-shaped and pointed at tips. Flowering stalk is leafless and may be shorter than leaves. Tiny flowers are densely packed. Corollas are 4-parted.

Bloom Time: April to September.

Habitat/Range: Desert shrublands to mountain brush communities up to 6,700', from British Columbia to Texas.

Comments: *Plantago* is from the Latin *planta* (sole of the foot), referring to the broad foot-shaped leaves of some species. *Patagonica* (of Patagonia) refers to the plant's distribution. Another common name is woolly plantain. Seeds have a mucilaginous coat and make a laxative when soaked in water and then consumed.

WATSON'S SLENDERLOBE
Leptodactylon watsonii
Phlox family (Polemoniaceae)

Description: Perennial, cushion-forming, mostly 4–20" wide. Leaves are 3- to 9-cleft, spiny, and opposite. White flowers have 6 greenish, unequal sepals and usually 4–6 petals that form a short tube and flare to ⅜–¾" wide at top.

Bloom Time: May to July.

Habitat/Range: Backbrush to mountain brush communities in the Intermountain West.

Comments: *Leptodactylon* is from the Greek *leptos* (thin) and *daktylos* (finger), referring to the narrow leaf segments. The flowers close up in the evening. *Watsonii* honors Sereno Watson (1826–1892), a collector and eventual curator of the Harvard herbarium.

CARPET PHLOX
Phlox hoodii
Phlox family (Polemoniaceae)

Description: Very low-growing perennial plant that forms cushions or matlike clusters, mainly 2–15" wide. Stems are covered with white hairs. Linear leaves are opposite, tightly arranged, and ⅛–¾" long with spiny tips. White, blue, or lavender flowers arise from hairy calyx. Corolla tube is ⅜–½" long and flares to 5 lobes. Fruit is a seed.

Bloom Time: March to June.

Habitat/Range: Desert shrub, pinyon-juniper, and ponderosa pine communities from Alaska to Colorado, 4,500–10,000' and up.

Comments: *Phlox* (flame) is in reference to the brightly colored flowers of many species. *Hoodii* honors Robert Hood (1797–1820), the map maker and artist on the Franklin Arctic Expedition of 1819–1822. *P. austromontana*, desert phlox, is similar but with larger flowers and more lightly colored leaves.

LONG-LEAF PHLOX
Phlox longifolia
Phlox family (Polemoniaceae)

Description: Perennial; stems solitary but may be clumped. Mainly 1⅛–16" tall, plants are woody below; linear to lance-shaped leaves are ⅜–3" long. Flowers are borne in loose clusters at ends of stems; central or terminal flower blooms first. Flowers are ⅜–¾" wide, with long corolla tube that is white, pink, or lavender.

Bloom Time: April to August.

Habitat/Range: Salt desert and mixed desert shrub communities up to the spruce fir communities across much of the West.

Comments: *Phlox* (flame) refers to the brightly colored flowers of many species. *Longifolia* (long-leaved) refers to the long, narrow leaves, which also inspired the common name.

FREMONT'S BUCKWHEAT
Eriogonum corymbosum
Buckwheat family (Polygonaceae)

Description: Clump-forming shrub, up to 4' tall and just as wide. Lance-shaped or elliptical leaves are ¼–1½" long and smooth or densely covered with hairs on one or both sides. Flat-topped cluster of small white flowers cloak plant. Flowers lack petals; petal-like sepals are ⅛–¼" long.

Bloom Time: July to October.

Habitat/Range: Variety of grassland and shrubland communities up to the pinyon-juniper community in the Southwest.

Comments: John C. Frémont collected this species in 1845 near Eagle County, Colorado. There are numerous varieties of this complex species. *Corymbosum* (corymbs) refers to the arrangement of flowers in flat-topped clusters known as corymbs. These striking shrubs bloom in late summer.

CUSHION BUCKWHEAT
Eriogonum ovalifolium
Buckwheat family (Polygonaceae)

Description: Mound-forming perennial, 2–16" across. Basal leaves are round or spatula-shaped and covered with woolly hairs. Leaf blades are ¾–2⅜" long, and petioles are up to 2" long. Leafless flowering stalks bear rounded cluster of small white flowers striped with purple; 6 petal-like segments are similar.

Bloom Time: March to July.

Habitat/Range: Shrublands to alpine communities across much of the West.

Comments: *Ovalifolium* (oval leaves) refers to the shape of the leaves. This is a highly variable species.

ALCOVE COLUMBINE
Aquilegia micrantha
Buttercup family (Ranunculaceae)

Description: Perennial, 1–3' tall; stems may be covered with sticky hairs. Leaves are mainly basal, 2 or 3 times divided, and rounded lobes of leaflets are cleft. Flowers are 1–3" long, white to cream, and have 5 petals that end with long, tubular spurs. Dried fruits split into 5 segments and bear numerous tiny seeds.

Bloom Time: April to July.

Habitat/Range: Hanging garden communities in Utah, Arizona, and New Mexico.

Comments: Found mainly in moist alcoves, this plant is endemic to the Colorado Plateau. *Aquilegia* (eagle) refers to the flower spurs, which resemble an eagle's talons. *Columbine* is from the Latin word for doves, in reference to the flowers resembling a flock of doves. Hummingbirds pollinate the flowers.

WHITE VIRGIN'S-BOWER
Clematis ligusticifolia
Buttercup family (Ranunculaceae)

Description: Perennial woody vine that may reach 30' or more in length. Compound leaves have 3–7 lance- or egg-shaped leaflets that may be toothed along edges. Small, inconspicuous flowers have white sepals but lack petals and may be few to many per flat-topped cluster. Seed heads are like cotton balls; each seed bears a long, hairy tail.

Bloom Time: June to September.

Habitat/Range: Riparian communities, 3,500–7,425', from British Columbia to New Mexico.

Comments: *Clematis* is the Greek name of a climbing plant, and *ligusticifolia* (with leaves like *Ligusticum*) refers to the leaves' resemblance to those of another plant. The leaves have a very peppery flavor.

BIRCHLEAF BUCKTHORN
Rhamnus betulifolia
Buckthorn family (Rhamnaceae)

Description: Shrub, 3–8' tall, with alternate elliptical or egg-shaped leaves. Leaf petioles are up to ¾" long with broad blades, 1–6" long, and prominent veins. Flat-topped clusters of small white flowers grow in angle between leaf and stem. Berry-like fruits are about ⅜" long and red at maturity.

Bloom Time: April to June.

Habitat/Range: Hanging garden or moist sites in southern Utah and the Southwest.

Comments: Shrub often grows in rock crevices. *Rhamnus* is the Greek name of the plant, and *betulaefolia* (birchlike leaves) refers to the leaves' resemblance to those of the birch.

UTAH SERVICEBERRY
Amelanchier utahensis
Rose family (Rosaceae)

Description: Low to large shrub, 1½–13' tall; reddish stems intricately branched. Oval to egg-shaped or elliptical leaves are ⅜–1⅛" long, finely toothed along margin mainly near tip, and mostly hairy on one or both sides. White or pinkish fragrant flowers, ⅜–¾" wide, with gaps between spatula-shaped petals. Berries are seedy and purplish to pinkish.

Bloom Time: May to July.

Habitat/Range: Variety of moist or dry sites from sagebrush to ponderosa pine communities from Washington to the Southwest.

Comments: Native Americans and early settlers added the mealy fruits to dried meat and animal fat to make pemmican. Derivation of *Amelanchier* is obscure; *utahensis* (of Utah) alludes to the first recorded specimen, which was from Washington County, Utah.

ALDER-LEAF MOUNTAIN MAHOGANY
Cercocarpus montanus
Rose family (Rosaceae)

Description: Shrub to small tree, 3–12' tall and densely branched. Inversely egg- or lance-shaped deciduous leaves have short stems and are up to 2" long. Leaf margins have rounded or sawlike teeth. Small flowers lack petals and have numerous stamens. Fruit is a seed with a long, twisted tail.

Bloom Time: May to July.

Habitat/Range: Mountain brush, pinyon-juniper, aspen, and mixed coniferous communities from Oregon to Mexico.

Comments: *Cercocarpus* (tailed fruit) refers to the long plumes on the seeds. *Montanus* (of the mountains) refers to the higher elevation occurrence of these shrubs. The strong branches were used to make fire sticks, digging tools, and arrow points. Native Puebloan tribes made a dye from boiled bark or roots. The sharp-pointed seeds stick into the ground; then, as the wind blows, the twisted tails help "corkscrew" the seeds into the ground. Dwarf mountain mahogany *(C. intricatus)* has linear, evergreen leaves.

APACHE PLUME
Fallugia paradoxa
Rose family (Rosaceae)

Description: Shrub with scaly bark, growing up to 6' tall. Wedge-shaped, alternate leaves are ¼–¾" long with 3–5 lobes, green and scaly above. White flowers, ½–1" across, have 5 sepals, 5 petals, and numerous stamens. Striking seeds have long, feather-like hairs.

Bloom Time: May to June.

Habitat/Range: Blackbrush to pinyon-juniper communities at 2,900–7,150', from California to Mexico.

Comments: *Fallugia* is for V. Fallugis, a nineteenth-century botanist and churchman. The strong wood has been used for arrow shafts and broom handles. The feathery seeds resembled the war headdress of the Apache Indian; hence the common name. *Paradoxa* (unusual) probably refers to the seed heads. The long seed tails aid in wind dispersal.

WILD CRAB APPLE
Peraphyllum ramosissimum
Rose family (Rosaceae)

Description: Deciduous, many-branched shrub that grows 4–7' tall and is nearly as broad. Alternate linear-shaped leaves are about ¾–1½" long and generally smooth along the margin. Blossoms are borne singularly or in small clusters with 2–5 white flowers that are about 1" wide. Yellowish-red fruits are ½" wide.

Bloom Time: May to July.

Habitat/Range: Rocky areas and cliff faces in pinyon-juniper and mountain brush habitats at 5,500–8,500', from Oregon to New Mexico.

Comments: Peraphyllum (very leafy) and ramosissimum (many-branched) define this plant. The small fruit, called a pome, is eaten by grouse, wild turkeys, small rodents, and black bears in the fall. Thomas Nuttall first collected this shrub while on the Nathaniel Wyeth Expedition (1834–1837) in Oregon. Also called Indian apple.

ROCK SPIREA
Petrophytum caespitosum
Rose family (Rosaceae)

Description: Mat-forming shrub up to 3' or more wide. Spatula- or inversely lance-shaped leaves, ⅛–¾" long, have long, straight hairs on one or both sides or are smooth. Flowers are arranged in dense cluster at end of short stem; tiny petals are white.

Bloom Time: July to October.

Habitat/Range: Rocky outcrops from sagebrush up to alpine communities or on ceilings of hanging garden communities from Oregon to New Mexico.

Comments: The shrub either forms a dense mat over the rock surface or hangs freely from an alcove wall attached only by the stout root. *Petrophytum* (rock plant) refers to its habit of growing on rock. *Caespitosum* (low-growing) refers to the matlike growth form.

CHOKECHERRY
Prunus virginiana
Rose family (Rosaceae)

Description: Tall shrub or small tree, up to 35' tall, but may form wide shrubs. Egg-shaped leaves are 1–5" long and nearly as wide, with toothed margins and pointed tips. Undersides of leaves may have some hairs. White flowers are borne in elongated dense clusters. Fruit is a black, tart berry.

Bloom Time: May to August.

Habitat/Range: Sagebrush slopes to pinyon-juniper woodlands up to aspen communities, 4,275–9,500', across much of North America.

Comments: *Prunus* (plum tree) refers to a group of fruit-bearing trees. *Virginiana* (of Virginia) refers to the location of the first discovered species. The tart fruit is consumed by wildlife and birds. Native Americans mixed chokecherry with meat and animal fat to make pemmican. The fruits were and still are collected to make jams and jellies.

CLIFFROSE
Purshia mexicana
Rose family (Rosaceae)

Description: Many-branched shrub with shredded bark, mainly 1½–8' tall. Leaves are ⅛–⅝" long, mostly 5-lobed, glandular dotted, and resinous. Flowers, ½–1" wide, are white to cream or yellowish with 5 petals and many stamens. Long-tailed hairs are attached to the seeds.

Bloom Time: May to August.

Habitat/Range: Mixed desert grassland-shrublands up to mountain brush communities throughout the Southwest.

Comments: Plants may be cloaked with fragrant flowers. *Purshia* is for Frederick T. Pursh (1774–1820), author of one of the earliest floras of North America. *Mexicana* refers to the range of the plant: Southwest to central Mexico. A refreshing tea may be made from the leaves.

BASTARD TOADFLAX
Comandra umbellata
Sandalwood family (Santalaceae)

Description: Semi-parasitic perennial, stems erect, and 3–13" tall. Linear, lance-shaped, or narrowly elliptical leaves are ⅜–1¼" long and smooth. Flowers lack petals; 5 sepals are whitish green. Purplish or brown fleshy layer coats the 1-seeded fruit.

Bloom Time: March to July.

Habitat/Range: Wide variety of shrublands to spruce fir communities at 2,650–9,900' across much of North America.

Comments: *Comandra* is from the Greek *kome* (hair) and *andros* (man); the stamens are hairy at their bases. *Umbellata* (umbel-like) refers to the flat-topped flower clusters. Known to parasitize over 200 plant species, bastard toadflax is also an alternate host for hard pine rust disease.

ABAJO PENSTEMON
Penstemon lentus
Figwort family (Scrophulariaceae)

Description: Perennial, 12–20" tall, with smooth stems. Basal leaves are spatula-shaped, ¾–4" long; stem leaves are broadly and inversely lance-shaped and stemless. Flowers are borne in leaf axils in clusters, white (on the west side of the Abajo Mountains) or blue to violet (on the east side of the Abajos). Corolla is tube-shaped, ½–1" long, and lobes spread flat at the opening.

Bloom Time: May to July.

Habitat/Range: Sagebrush, pinyon-juniper, and ponderosa pine communities in southeastern Utah, Colorado, and Arizona.

Comments: A Colorado Plateau endemic, the variety *albiflorus* is found on the west side of the Abajo Mountains and near Natural Bridges National Monument. *Albiflorus* (white flower) refers to the flower color and another common name for the plant: whiteflower penstemon.

SACRED DATURA
Datura wrightii
Potato family (Solanaceae)

Description: Annual or perennial, often in rounded clumps, 1–4½' tall, and covered with dense, fine gray hairs. Large leaves, 2–10" long, have egg-shaped blades, toothed along margins, with short white hairs. Green sepals have lance-shaped lobes. Whitish to violet trumpet-shaped corollas are 5–9" long and about as wide. Golfball-shaped fruit is covered with prickles.

Bloom Time: May to September.

Habitat/Range: Blackbrush to pinyon-juniper communities from California to Mexico.

Comments: A poisonous narcotic plant, it was formerly used to induce visions. The large flowers open in the evening and are pollinated by a host of night-flying insects and moths. *Wrightii* honors Charles Wright, who first collected this plant in Texas in 1850.

INDIAN TOBACCO
Nicotiana attenuata
Potato family (Solanaceae)

Description: Annual plant, 1–3' tall, with sticky hairs on stems. Leaves are elliptical to broadly lance-shaped and ½–2" long. Trumpet or funnel-shaped flowers are 1–2" long with lobes flaring open at tips. Fruit is a small capsule containing tiny seeds.

Bloom Time: June to August.

Habitat/Range: Disturbed sites from Idaho to Texas and California.

Comments: *Nicotiana* honors Jean Nicot de Villemain (1530–1600), a French ambassador to Portugal who is credited with introducing tobacco plants into France in the sixteenth century. *Attenuata* (pointed) refers to the pointed sepal tips. Native Americans harvested and smoked this plant. Indian tobacco, also called coyote tobacco, grows in disturbed sites.

TAMARISK
Tamarix chinensis
Tamarisk family (Tamaricaceae)

Description: Shrub to moderately sized tree, with reddish-brown bark and intricate branching. Scale-like leaves are minute and juniper-like. Fragrant, white to pinkish flowers are borne in elongated clusters; flowers have 5 sepals and 5 petals.

Bloom Time: May to July.

Habitat/Range: Moist sites or riparian communities along streams and rivers throughout the Southwest.

Comments: Introduced from Eurasia for erosion control in the West, tamarisk spread to Utah around 1880 and by the 1920s was established along the Colorado River and its tributaries. Tamarisk is named for the Tamaris River in Spain; *chinensis* (of China) refers to its Eurasian distribution. Beetles native to Eurasia have been used in biological pest control programs to eradicate different species of tamarisk from the Southwest.

YELLOW FLOWERS

This section includes yellow, golden, and yellowish-orange flowers. Some flowers have mixed colors, especially the members of the sunflower family, whose ray and disk flowers are often different colors; they are included in this section.

SKUNKBUSH
Rhus aromatica
Cashew family (Anacardiaceae)

Description: Compact, densely branched shrub mainly 2–8' tall. Branchlets are brown and flexible, becoming gray with age. Leaves are simple and lobed or separated into 3 leaflets; leaflets are lobed and smooth or minutely hairy on one or both sides. Tiny yellowish flowers arranged in dense clusters along short branches appear before leaves in early spring. Fruit is a hard, lentil-size seed within a fleshy reddish-orange covering.

Bloom Time: March to May.

Habitat/Range: Riparian and moist sites to pinyon-juniper communities in the Southwest and north to Iowa.

Comments: Native Americans still collect the supple, grayish branchlets for their basketry. The crushed leaves have a disagreeable odor; hence the common name. Fruits are high in vitamin C, and a refreshing but sour drink can be made by soaking the seeds in water. Wildlife eat the berries.

FENDLER'S CYMOPTERUS
Cymopterus acaulis
Carrot family (Apiaceae)

Description: Common low-growing perennial plant, 2¾–9" tall. Leaves spread laterally along ground and are 2–3 times divided into lobes that are also deeply divided. Leaf petioles are 1–4" long, and blades are about as long. Small, sticky hairs on leaves and stems are often coated with sand grains. Clusters of small, yellowish flowers are arranged at ends of leafless stem. Tiny petals are yellow, white, or purplish. Seeds are ¼" long with crinkled wings that are somewhat corky.

Bloom Time: March to June.

Habitat/Range: Desert shrub, sagebrush, and pinyon-juniper woodlands, often in sandy soils, 4,360–9,000' throughout the Southwest.

Comments: *Cymopterus* (wavy wing) refers to the wavy margin along the winged fruits. *Acaulis* (without a stem) describes the lack of a stem. The parsnip-like taproot can be eaten raw or cooked. This plant has also been known as *C. fendleri* in honor of August Fendler, a nineteenth-century plant collector.

CANYONLANDS BISCUITROOT
Lomatium latilobum
Carrot family (Apiaceae)

Description: Perennial plant, 4–20" tall, often in dense clumps growing from branched woody base. Leaves are divided into 3–4 pairs of lateral, dull green elliptical leaflets that may be lobed or toothed. Flower stalks are smooth and 1½–10½" tall. Short stems bear flat-topped clusters of yellowish flowers that arise from common point. Seeds are flat and wide with lateral wings.

Bloom Time: April to June.

Habitat/Range: Generally in association with the Entrada Sandstone in southeastern Utah and southwestern Colorado.

Comments: A Colorado Plateau endemic, biscuitroot grows mostly in Arches National Park and Colorado National Monument. Native Americans ate the roots raw or pulverized them into flour; hence the common name. *Lomatium* (fringed) refers to the winged fruit, and *latilobum* (broad lobes) refers to the shape of the leaf.

PARRY'S LOMATIUM
Lomatium parryi
Carrot family (Apiaceae)

Description: Perennial, 3–16" tall, arising from short, branched woody base. Leaves are highly dissected, dark green, and with 7–9 opposite pairs of primary leaflets branching from main leaf stem. Reddish when young, leafless flower stalks are 2–24" tall, topped by cluster of tiny yellow flowers that turn white with age. Seeds are ½" long, flattened, and with lateral wings.

Bloom Time: February to May.

Habitat/Range: Blackbrush and pinyon-juniper communities from Utah to California.

Comments: Flowers bloom before the leaves develop; the previous season's dried leaves may still be present when the plant blooms. *Parryi* is in honor of Charles Christopher Parry (1823–1890), an American botanist who was the first official botanist of the USDA. Parry made notable botanical surveys of the American West and discovered numerous plants.

NINE-LEAF BISCUITROOT
Lomatium triternatum
Carrot family (Apiaceae)

Description: Perennial, 1–2' tall, arising from stout root. Compound leaves are dissected into 3 segments that are in turn divided into narrow, linear segments ½–5" long. Flowers are borne in small clusters arranged to form larger flat-topped cluster. Individual flowers are yellow and very small. Fruit is a flattened seed with papery wings and ribs.

Bloom Time: April to June.

Habitat/Range: Moist to dry sites in meadows or slopes in sagebrush flats, pinyon-juniper woodlands, mountain brush, and ponderosa pine communities, 4,000–9,000', from British Columbia to Colorado.

Comments: *Lomatium* (a border or edge) refers to the dorsal ribs or papery wings that adorn seeds in this genus. *Triternatum* (triply ternate) describes the highly divided leaves.

LOUISIANA WORMWOOD

Artemisia ludoviciana
Sunflower family (Asteraceae)

Description: Perennial herb to 3' tall, often growing in dense clusters. Stemless leaves are narrow, up to 4" long, pointed at tips, and densely covered with white hairs on undersides. Leaves range from green to white on upper surface and may be lobed or toothed along edges. Numerous small, yellowish flower heads occur along an elongated stem.

Bloom Time: June to October.

Habitat/Range: Variety of habitats throughout the West and Midwest.

Comments: A fragrant plant, *Ludoviciana* means "of St. Louis"; the plant was first recorded there by Thomas Nuttall (1786–1859), a botanist and naturalist who traveled in the western frontier.

BUDSAGE

Artemisia spinescens
Sunflower family (Asteraceae)

Description: Low shrub to about 1' tall. After blooming, when flowers have fallen, stems become 1" spines. Leaves are ¼–¾" long, grayish hairy, and finely divided into 5–7 3-parted lobes. Flower heads are yellow, about ¼" high and wide, and made of 6–20 flowers or more. Outer disk flowers are fertile; inner ones are sterile.

Bloom Time: March to July.

Habitat/Range: Variety of soil types in shrublands, 3,700–6,000', from Oregon to New Mexico.

Comments: Budsage often grows in saline soils. The common name is derived from the clusters of leaves and flowers, which resemble buds. *Spinescens* (spiny) refers to the inch-long spines. Budsage recovers quickly from overbrowsing.

BIG SAGEBRUSH
Artemisia tridentata
Sunflower family (Asteraceae)

Description: Shrub, averaging 2–7" tall, with stout trunk and shaggy bark. Leaves are silver-gray, hairy, wedge-shaped, ¼–2" long, and 3- to 5-toothed at tips. Non-lobed leaves may appear in early winter. Flowering stems generally surpass vegetative branches and contain numerous side branches that bear dense clusters of tiny flower heads. Flowers have yellow to cream corollas. Seeds are tiny, black, and smooth.

Bloom Time: June to October.

Habitat/Range: Vast acreages in the arid West, up to 7,500'.

Comments: The most common sagebrush of the mesa and plains habitat in the Southwest, it is also the state flower of Nevada. *Tridentata* (3-toothed) refers to the typical 3 lobes on the leaves, which are very fragrant.

ARROWLEAF BALSAMROOT
Balsamorhiza sagittata
Sunflower family (Asteraceae)

Description: Large perennial, ½–2' tall and about as wide. Large arrow-shaped leaves may reach 10" in length and 6" wide. Leaf margins are smooth. Flowering stalks arise from base of leaves and bear yellow flower heads, 2–4" wide. Both ray and disk flowers are present. Fruit is a seed.

Bloom Time: May to July.

Habitat/Range: Dry sites in sagebrush flats, mountain brush, pinyon-juniper woodlands, and ponderosa pine forests, 4,100–9,425', across the western United States and British Columbia.

Comments: Perennials may color a hill or sagebrush flat with their blooms. *Balsamorhiza* (balsam root) refers to the aroma of the roots resembling balsawood. *Sagitatta* (arrow-shaped) refers to the outline of the leaves. Native Americans harvested the young roots and shoots in spring as a food source or for their medicinal properties. Deer and elk browse on this plant.

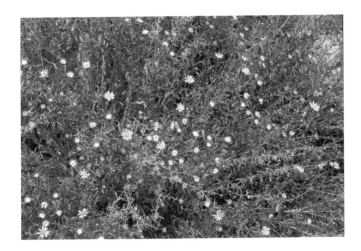

HAIRY GOLDENASTER
Chrysopsis villosa
Sunflower family (Asteraceae)

Description: Perennial with several to many stems, often forming sprawling clumps 7–20" tall. Inversely lance-shaped to elliptical leaves have moderately stiff hairs. Flower heads, ½" wide, are few to numerous per flowering stalk; each head has 10–25 yellow rays, ¼–⅜" long, that surround compact cluster of yellow disk flowers. Seeds are tipped with white, hairy bristles.

Bloom Time: April to August.

Habitat/Range: Blackbrush to ponderosa pine communities across the western United States.

Comments: *Villosa* (soft-hairy) refers to the gray hairs on the leaves and stems; another name is *Heterotheca villosa*. The golden-yellow flower heads resemble those of an aster; hence the common name.

RUBBER RABBITBRUSH
Chrysothamnus nauseosus
Sunflower family (Asteraceae)

Description: Shrub, 1–7' tall; bark obscured by dense, woolly covering of hairs. Leaves are linear and flat, up to 4" long, hairy or smooth, and narrow at tips. Flower heads are numerous and arranged in flat-topped clusters at terminal ends of branches. Disk flowers are yellow to yellow-orange. Small seeds have numerous bristles.

Bloom Time: June to October.

Habitat/Range: Depending on variety, found throughout the West, 3,330–7,720'.

Comments: *Chrysothamnus* is from the Greek *chrysos* (golden) and *thamos* (a shrub). *Nauseosus* (heavy-scented) refers to the smell of the leaves and flowers. The flowers make a bright yellow dye; a latex, used in manufacturing rubber, also comes from the plant. There are many varieties of *C. nauseosus*, which is also called chamissa.

BUSH ENCELIA
Encelia frutescens
Sunflower family (Asteraceae)

Description: Bushy shrub, 1–4' tall, with erect stems. Leaves are up to 1" long, alternate and toothed or entire along margins, egg-shaped to rounded or lance-shaped, with stiff hairs that lie close against surface. Showy flowers are ⅜–1⅜" wide and solitary. Yellow ray flowers may be lacking or, on average, 1–16 or possibly more, ⅜" long, and surrounding dense cluster of yellow disk flowers.

Bloom Time: May to July.

Habitat/Range: Rocky areas in blackbrush and pinyon-juniper communities in southeastern Utah and Arizona.

Comments: *Encelia* is in honor of Christopher Encel, a sixteenth-century botanist. *Frutescens* (becoming shrubby) refers to the woody nature of the plant. The resin that exudes from the stem of a related plant, brittlebush (*E. farinosa*), was burned as incense by Spanish priests in the Southwest, which gave rise to another common name: incienso. Native Americans chewed the resin for pain relief.

NAKEDSTEM
Enceliopsis nudicaulis
Sunflower family (Asteraceae)

Description: Perennial, 4–24" tall, with leafless flowering stalks arising from woody base. Stout stem has dense, white hairs. Broadly rounded to egg-shaped leaves have long petioles and are covered with fine, silvery hairs around stem base. Solitary, coarse flower heads are ¾" high and over 2" wide. Each head has 13–21 yellow rays that surround dense cluster of yellow disk flowers.

Bloom Time: April to July.

Habitat/Range: Blackbrush to pinyon-juniper communities in the Southwest to California.

Comments: *Enceliopsis* (similar to *Encelia*) refers to the resemblance to another genus in the Asteraceae. *Nudicaulis* (naked stem) refers to the leafless flowering stalk. The related *E. nutans*, noddinghead, has flat, rounded leaves and a solitary flower head that is rayless.

HOPI BLANKETFLOWER
Gaillardia pinnatifida
Sunflower family (Asteraceae)

Description: Perennial, 3⅛–22" tall, generally bearing leaves halfway up stem. Hairy leaves, up to 3" long, are usually lobed or wavy; lobes may reach halfway to midrib of blade. Solitary flower heads on long stems have 7–12 yellow rays that surround dense cluster of brownish-purple disk flowers. Rays are often 3-lobed; entire flower head has some long, soft hairs.

Bloom Time: April to July.

Habitat/Range: Across the Southwest in blackbrush, mixed shrub-grassland, and pinyon-juniper communities, 2,270–6,500'.

Comments: *Gaillardia* is for M. Gaillard de Charentoreau, an eighteenth-century French magistrate and patron of botany. *Pinnatifida* (pinnately lobed; cleft leaves) describes the leaves. The Hopi used the plant as a diuretic.

ERECT GUMWEED
Grindelia fastigiata
Sunflower family (Asteraceae)

Description: Perennial with smooth stems averaging 2–4' tall. Leaves, ½–5⅛" long, are inversely lance- to broadly lance-shaped, with margins entire or toothed. Flower heads, ½" wide, are primarily disk flowers but may have outer row of small yellow ray flowers. Bracts that subtend flower heads are in 6 rows; some rows are bent outward. Bracts and flowers are sticky to the touch.

Bloom Time: June to October.

Habitat/Range: Mixed desert shrub, riparian, mountain brush, and disturbed sites in the Southwest and Great Plains.

Comments: *Grindelia* is for David Hieronymus Grindel (1776–1836), a professor in Riga, Latvia. *Fastigiata* refers to the upright, clustered branches. Gumweed is a source of grindelia, a spasmodic used medicinally to stimulate the mucous membranes in the treatment of chronic bronchitis and asthma. *G. squarrosa*, curlycup gumweed, is similar but has large ray flowers and strongly curled involucre bracts.

THRIFTY GOLDENWEED
Haplopappus armeroides
Sunflower family (Asteraceae)

Description: Low-growing perennial arising from stout root. Dried and withered leaves remain attached to lower stems, while green leaves are ½–4" long and linear in shape. Leaf tips have short point. Flowering stems are mostly leafless or bear smaller leaves toward flowering head. Heads bear both yellow disk and ray flowers; 8–12 rays are about ½" long. Fruit is a seed with silky hairs.

Bloom Time: May to July.

Habitat/Range: Sandy or gravelly soils in desert shrub, pinyon-juniper, and mountain brush communities, 3,700–7,550', from Montana south to Arizona and New Mexico and east to Nebraska.

Comments: *Armeroides* (similar to *Armeria*) indicates this plant's similarity to another genus. The plants grow outward in a ring pattern and, as they age, die off in the center. Another species name is *Stenotus armeroides.*

ORANGE SNEEZEWEED
Helenium hoopesii
Sunflower family (Asteraceae)

Description: Perennial herb growing 10–40" high. Hairy basal leaves, 1–15" long, have parallel veins and nearly white midvein. Flowering stem leaves are smaller and lance- to egg-shaped. Flowers are arranged in loose flat-top clusters with 2–11 individual flowering heads. Each flowering head bears both ray and disk flowers; 13–22 rays are yellow to orangish, separated from each other, and ¾–1½" long. Disk flowers are arranged in a mound. Hairy fruit is a seed.

Bloom Time: June to August.

Habitat/Range: Sagebrush meadows, mountain brush communities, and up to aspen forests in moist sites from Oregon to the Southwest.

Comments: *Helenium* (Helen of Troy) comes from the name of another plant. *Hoopesii* honors Thomas Hoops (1834–1925), an explorer and seed collector in Colorado. Another species name is *Dugaldia hoopesii*.

PRAIRIE SUNFLOWER
Helianthus petiolaris
Sunflower family (Asteraceae)

Description: Annual, 2–48" tall, stems smooth or covered with short, stiff hairs. Alternate leaves are petioled, with blades up to 3⅛" long and lance-shaped to round in outline. Leaf margins entire or with some serrations bear short, stiff hairs. Flower heads solitary or several per stalk, 2–4" wide, have yellow ray flowers surrounding cluster of brownish-purple disk flowers.

Bloom Time: April to September.

Habitat/Range: Grasslands to mountain brush communities, often in disturbed sites; widespread in the United States and Canada.

Comments: *Helianthus* (sunflower) refers to the flower's habit of turning with the sun. *Petiolaris* (with a petiole) refers to the stalked leaf. Sunflower seeds are consumed by small rodents and birds.

COMMON HYALINEHERB
Hymenopappus filifolius
Sunflower family (Asteraceae)

Description: Perennial, with clustered smooth or woolly stems, growing 2–24" high or taller. Basal leaves are finely dissected, grayish hairy, and 1⅛–8" long; upper leaves smaller or lacking. Flower heads are solitary or in small clusters, conical to bell-shaped, with 10–59 yellow disk flowers per head.

Bloom Time: May to July.

Habitat/Range: Variety of desert shrub to ponderosa pine communities in the Southwest.

Comments: *Hymenopappus* is from the Greek *hymen* (membrane) and *pappus* (down), referring to the membranous scales on the crown of the seed. *Filifolius* (threadlike leaves) refers to the fine divisions of the leaf blade.

STEMLESS WOOLLYBASE
Hymenoxys acaulis
Sunflower family (Asteraceae)

Description: Perennial. Leaves are basal; mostly leafless flower stalk, up to 2' tall, is smooth or has soft hairs. Narrow basal leaves, ⅜–2⅜" long, sometimes end in short, abrupt tips. Stem leaves, if present, are few and small. Flower heads are solitary or in pairs; bracts that subtend flower head are in 2–3 unequal series. Ray flowers, 5–9, are lobed at tips and surround small cluster of yellow disk flowers.

Bloom Time: April to July.

Habitat/Range: Mixed desert shrub and pinyon-juniper communities in the Southwest.

Comments: *Hymenoxys* is from the Greek *hymen* (membrane) and *oxys* (sharp), in reference to the pointed pappus scales. *Acaulis* (without a stem) refers to the very short woody base of the plant. Native Americans made a stimulating beverage from the leaves and also applied the leaves as a local anesthetic.

81

SOWTHISTLE DESERT DANDELION
Malacothrix sonchoides
Sunflower family (Asteraceae)

Description: Annual, 2–14" tall, with stems often branching from base. Stems are smooth or have short, yellowish glandular hairs. Basal leaves, up to 4½" long and 1" wide, are deeply divided with toothed lobes. Flower heads are solitary or few per cluster, about ½" across, and ray flowers are 5-lobed; lacks disk flowers.

Bloom Time: May to July.

Habitat/Range: Blackbrush to pinyon-juniper communities from California to New Mexico.

Comments: *Malacothrix* is from the Greek *malakos* (soft) and *thrix* (hair), referring to the soft hairs of the pappus. *Sonchoides* (similar to *Sonchus*) refers to the flower's resemblance to those in the *Sonchus* genus.

ROCK GOLDENROD

Petradoria pumila
Sunflower family (Asteraceae)

Description: Perennial, with numerous clustered stems 3–12" long. Base is covered with dark to ash withered leaves. Leathery leaves, 1–5" long, are linear to elliptical to lance-shaped and clustered at base of stems; stem leaves are smaller. Clusters of 2–8 yellow flower heads, ¼" wide, have 1–3 ray flowers and are arranged in flat-topped pattern.

Bloom Time: June to September.

Habitat/Range: Mixed desert shrub up to ponderosa pine communities from Idaho to New Mexico.

Comments: *Petradoria* (rock-growing) refers to its habit of growing on or near rock surfaces. *Pumila* (dwarf) refers to the short stature of the plant.

NAKEDSTEM BAHIA

Platyschkuhria integrifolia
Sunflower family (Asteraceae)

Description: Perennial, stems solitary or few; individual plants may be clustered. Stems are 4½–24" tall with white hairs. Main leaves near base are petioled, blades ½–4" long, and egg- to lance-shaped. Flower heads grow 2–10 per stem; 7–11 yellow ray flowers surround cluster of yellow disk flowers.

Bloom Time: May to July.

Habitat/Range: Clay soils in desert shrub, pinyon-juniper, and mountain brush communities in the Southwest.

Comments: The common name was inspired by the leafless flowering stem. *Platyschuhria* comes from the Greek *platy* (broad) and *schkuhria* (another Asteraceae genus).

WOOLLY PAPERFLOWER
Psilostrophe tagetina
Sunflower family (Asteraceae)

Description: Perennial, often forming round bushes. Stems, 5½–24" tall, are moderately to densely hairy at bases, less so upward. Leaves, ½" long, are narrow, linear, or spatula-shaped. Flower heads, ⅜–¾" wide, usually have 3–6 yellow ray flowers surrounding 6 yellow disk flowers.

Bloom Time: May to October.

Habitat/Range: Salt desert shrub and pinyon-juniper communities in southeastern Utah and south to Mexico.

Comments: The common name comes from the ray flowers, which become papery when mature. Greenstem paperflower (*P. sparsiflora*) has green stems. All species of paperflower in the Four Corners region are toxic to livestock.

UINTA GROUNDSEL
Senecio multilobatus
Sunflower family (Asteraceae)

Description: Perennial, with stems mainly 4–24" tall and several stems per plant. Basal leaves are spatula- to egg-shaped and deeply dissected; lobes are irregularly toothed or rounded. Flower heads, ⅜–1" wide, are in flat-topped clusters, with 7–13 narrow yellow ray flowers that surround dense cluster of yellowish disk flowers. Seeds have white hairs.

Bloom Time: May to July.

Habitat/Range: Blackbrush up to spruce-fir communities from Wyoming to New Mexico.

Comments: *Senecio* is from the Latin *senex* (old man), referring to the fluffy white hairs on the seeds, which resemble an old man's beard. *Multilobatus* (many-lobed) describes the leaves. Senecios hybridize across species lines and at times make identification difficult.

BROOM GROUNDSEL
Senecio spartoides
Sunflower family (Asteraceae)

Description: Perennial, 8–40" tall, stems stout and often in clumps. Smooth leaves, ¾–4" long, are linear, mostly undivided, and along entire stem. Flower heads are few to many in flat-topped clusters; each head is ⅜–1" wide and has 4–8 yellow ray flowers surrounding small cluster of yellow disk flowers. Seeds have bright white hairs.

Bloom Time: June to October.

Habitat/Range: Warm desert shrub, pinyon-juniper, and aspen communities in the Southwest.

Comments: This colorful plant blooms in late summer. *Senecio* is derived from a word meaning "old man" and refers to the white hairs on the pappus resembling white whiskers. *Spartoides* (similar to *Spartium*) refers to the plant's similarity to another genus in the pea family.

COMMON GOLDENROD
Solidago canadensis
Sunflower family (Asteraceae)

Description: Perennial, with stems 1–5' tall or more. Stems are minutely downy in at least upper half and smooth below. Stem leaves are narrow, possibly sharp-toothed along margins, ¾–4" long, and show three distinct veins. Flower heads are borne on one side of curved stem. Individual heads are small; 10–17 yellowish ray flowers surround tiny cluster of yellowish disk flowers.

Bloom Time: May to September.

Habitat/Range: Riparian and moist sites across much of North America.

Comments: *Solidago* (to make whole) refers to the healing properties of goldenrod; a tea brewed from the leaves was used for intestinal fever. Flowers make a yellow dye. *Canadensis* (of Canada) refers to the plant's type locality.

INDIAN TEA
Thelesperma megapotamicum
Sunflower family (Asteraceae)

Description: Perennial herb with stems 15–40" tall. Leaves are opposite, 1–3" long, and once or twice divided; upper leaves are linear. Flower stalks are leafless with heads ¼–¾" wide. Small outer bracts below heads are egg-shaped and bent. Ray flowers are usually lacking. Disk flowers are yellow or brownish. Seeds have 2 hairs.

Bloom Time: May to September.

Habitat/Range: Desert shrub and ponderosa pine communities from Wyoming to Mexico and in South America.

Comments: Dried flowers and young leaves make an excellent tea; another common name is Navajo tea. *Thelesperma* is from the Greek *thele* (nipple) and *sperma* (seed), in reference to the small pointed projections on the seeds. Scapose greenthread *(T. subnudum)* has bright yellow ray flowers and opposite leaves.

YELLOW SALSIFY
Tragopogon dubius
Sunflower family (Asteraceae)

Description: Biennial, with erect stems 1–3½' tall. Leaves are grasslike, linear, 2–10" long, and may have loose tufts of woolly hairs. Flower stalk is inflated below flowering head; long pointed bracts below flowering head are longer than lemon-yellow ray flowers. Disk flowers are yellow. Flower head becomes airy globe, 3–4" wide, of long whitish hairs attached to the seeds.

Bloom Time: May to September.

Habitat/Range: Across a wide elevational range in a variety of habitats throughout much of the United States. Native to Europe.

Comments: *Tragopogon* is from the Greek *tragos* (goat) and *pogon* (beard) because the flower head bracts resemble a goat's beard. Roots were soaked to remove the bitterness, then peeled and eaten raw or stewed; their flavor is similar to that of oysters. Another common name is oyster-plant.

ROUGH MULESEARS
Wyethia scabra
Sunflower family (Asteraceae)

Description: Perennial, often in dense, sprawling clumps, 1–3' tall and as wide or wider. Stems and leaves are covered with rough, stiff hairs. Leaves are linear to elliptical, 1–7" long. Flower heads, 1–3" wide, are generally solitary at terminal ends of branches. Yellow elliptical rays, 10–23, surround dense cluster of yellow disk flowers.

Bloom Time: May to July.

Habitat/Range: Sandier soils in blackbrush, mixed desert shrub, pinyon-juniper woodlands, and ponderosa pine up to 8,100' in Four Corners area and Wyoming.

Comments: Named for Nathaniel Wyeth (1802–1856), a Massachusetts businessman who led 2 overland expeditions to Oregon in 1832 and 1834. The botanist Thomas Nuttall and the ornithologist John Kirk Townsend accompanied the second expedition, during which Nuttall named this plant for Wyeth. *Scabra* (rough) refers to the texture of the leaves.

COCKLEBUR
Xanthium strumarium
Sunflower family (Asteraceae)

Description: Annual with rough-hairy, mottled purple stems, 7–40" tall or taller. Oval to egg-shaped or triangular leaves arise on long petioles and are ¾–5" long; leaf margins are toothed with many lobes. Yellow flower heads are few to many in small clusters that arise in angle between stem and leaves. Seedpod, ⅜–1½" long, is covered with stout, hooked prickles.

Bloom Time: June to October.

Habitat/Range: Moist areas in disturbed sites. Possibly native to the eastern United States.

Comments: *Xanthium* is the Greek name for the plant. *Strumarium* (rough) refers to either the texture of the stems or the burrs. Seedlings are poisonous to livestock and may cause a skin rash on people.

FREMONT'S MAHONIA
Mahonia fremontii
Barberry family (Berberidaceae)

Description: Evergreen shrub, 4–5' or taller, with spreading branches. Compound leaves have 3–9 bluish-green smooth leaflets, 1" long. Leaflets have 5–7 broad, triangular spine-tipped teeth or lobes. Yellow flowers, ½" wide, have 6 petals. Fruits are purplish or reddish seedy berries.

Bloom Time: April to June.

Habitat/Range: Desert shrub to mountain brush communities, 2,550–7,425', in the Four Corners region.

Comments: *Mahonia* is for Bernard M'Mahon (1755–1816), an Irish immigrant to the United States who ran a plant nursery in Philadelphia. Flowers are very fragrant and berries are edible. Pulverized roots make a yellow dye. *Fremontii* is for the explorer John C. Frémont, who collected the type specimen in Nevada.

RAVEN TENNYSON

YELLOW CRYPTANTH
Cryptantha flava
Borage family (Boraginaceae)

Description: Perennial, 4–16" tall, often with clustered stems. Foliage, flower stems, and sepals are densely covered with stiff hairs. Linear or inversely lance-shaped leaves are ¾–3" long and mainly basal. Dense clusters of yellow flowers, ¼" wide, have 5 petals that flare open at top of short tube. Small, arching crests encircle open mouth of tube.

Bloom Time: March to July.

Habitat/Range: Desert shrub, sagebrush, and pinyon-juniper communities up to 8,110' in eastern half of Utah and into Colorado, New Mexico, and Arizona.

Comments: *Cryptantha* is from the Greek *krypto* (to hide) and *anthos* (flower), in reference to the bracts obscuring the flowers on some of the species. *Flava* (yellow) describes the flower color.

SHOWY STONESEED
Lithospermum incisum
Borage family (Boraginaceae)

Description: Low-growing perennial, but may reach 20" tall. Dark green linear leaves, up to 3" long, have small hairs pressed close to surface. Each trumpet-shaped yellow flower has long, thin corolla tube that flares into 5 ruffled lobes. Flowers are 1" wide, and toothed lobes have fine hairs. Fruit is a hard, white nutlet.

Bloom Time: March to June.

Habitat/Range: Rocky soils in pinyon-juniper, sagebrush, and ponderosa pine communities, 4,200–8,950', in central United States and Mexico into Canada.

Comments: *Lithospermum* (stone seed) refers to the hard nutlet. *Incisum* (toothed) refers to the lobes of the flowers. Stimulating teas were made from stems, leaves, and roots.

89

WESTERN PUCCOON
Lithospermum ruderale
Borage family (Boraginaceae)

Description: Perennial with numerous stems arising from woody root, 1–2' tall. Upper leaves are linear and 1–4" long; lower leaves are smaller. Small trumpet-shaped yellow flowers, ½" wide, are borne at stem tips and nearly obscured by upper leaves. Fruit is a hard nutlet.

Bloom Time: May to August.

Habitat/Range: Dry foothills and plains in sagebrush, mountain brush, and ponderosa pine communities from California to western Colorado.

Comments: *Ruderale* (rubbish) refers to the plant's growth in disturbed sites. The Plains Indians harvested the roots as a food source and to make a remedy for respiratory illnesses. *Puccoon* is a Native word for dye plants; several species of stoneseed yield a purplish dye. This plant is also known as Western stoneseed.

NEWBERRY'S TWINPOD
Physaria newberryi
Mustard family (Brassicaceae)

Description: Low-growing perennial, 1–9" tall, with withered leaves attached to base. Basal leaves, up to 3" long, have rounded blades, egg- or spatula-shaped, with small point at tip. Leaves along flowering stalk are smaller. Yellow flowers, each with short flower stalk, are in tight clusters. Each flower has 4 spatula-shaped petals and is ¼–½" wide. Inflated seedpod has deep indentation between two halves.

Bloom Time: February to July.

Habitat/Range: Dry sandy to rocky soils in desert shrub, pinyon-juniper, and ponderosa pine communities in southern Utah, Arizona, and New Mexico.

Comments: *Physaria* is from the Greek *physa* (bladder), referring to the inflated seedpod. Twinpod comes from the seedpod's shape, which is like two balloons glued together. The species was named for John Strong Newberry (1822–1892), professor of geology at Columbia University, who also served on the Ives Expedition (1857–1858) to the Southwest and is credited as being the first geologist to visit the Grand Canyon.

WALLFLOWER
Erysimum asperum
Mustard family (Brassicaceae)

Description: Perennial or biennial, 6–30" tall. Basal leaves up to 4" long are linear, elliptical, or spatula-shaped. Leaf margins may be toothed, and surface has fine Y-shaped hairs. Stem leaves are linear, up to 4" long, with toothed margins. Flower stem bears dense clusters of yellow or yellowish-orange flowers that are ¾" wide and have 4 petals. Seedpods are up to 4" long.

Bloom Time: March to June.

Habitat/Range: Sandy or rocky soils across a wide elevational range from the Yukon to the Midwest.

Comments: This species demonstrates the greatest ecological distribution of all Utah plants, growing from 2,490' to 12,467' in elevation. *Erysimum* (help or save) refers to the plant's reported beneficial use. Wallflower is also known as *E. capitatum* in many areas.

COLORADO BLADDERPOD
Physaria rectipes
Mustard family (Brassicaceae)

Description: Perennial with low-growing or erect stems up to 16" long that arise from woody base. Base may have withered leaves. Basal leaves are elliptical or inversely lance-shaped, up to 3" long, and smooth or toothed along margins. Leaves along flowering stem are few and linear. Yellow flowers, with 4 petals, are about ½" wide. Fruits are rounded to elliptical inflated pods.

Bloom Time: April to July.

Habitat/Range: Blackbrush to ponderosa pine communities in sandy to rocky soils throughout the Southwest.

Comments: A former name was *Lesquerella,* in honor of Leo Lesquereux, a late-nineteenth-century American paleobotanist. *Physaria* (bladder) refers to the inflated seedpods.

TUMBLING MUSTARD
Sisymbrium altissimum
Mustard family (Brassicaceae)

Description: Annual weed, 10–40" tall, with coarse stiff hairs near base but smooth above. Basal leaves are lobed or highly divided and ⅜–8" long. Upper leaves are linear and threadlike. Four-petaled yellow flowers, ⅛–¼" wide, are borne on short stems. Long, narrow pod curves upward.

Bloom Time: March to September.

Habitat/Range: Disturbed sites throughout much of North America. Native to Europe.

Comments: The wind uproots the mature, dry plant and blows it across the land, scattering seeds like a tumbleweed. Seeds and young plants are edible. *Altissimum* (very tall) refers to the stature of this weed.

PRINCE'S PLUME
Stanleya pinnata
Mustard family (Brassicaceae)

Description: Long-plumed perennial that branches near base and has stems up to 4' tall. Lower leaves are deeply dissected, ½–6" long and ¾–1½" wide. Upper leaves are narrowly lance-shaped or elliptical. Elongated flowering stalk bears clusters of lacy yellow flowers, ¾–1½" long, with stamens protruding above 4 petals. Seedpods are long-stalked, narrow, and up to 3" long.

Bloom Time: May to August.

Habitat/Range: Selenium-bearing soil in desert shrub to mountain brush communities throughout the Intermountain West.

Comments: *Stanleya* is for Lord Edward Stanley (1755–1851), president of the Linnaean and Zoological societies in London. *Pinnata* (pinnate) refers to the deeply dissected leaves. Presence of this species indicates selenium-bearing soil and is toxic to livestock; however, native bighorn sheep forage on this plant.

COMMON PRICKLYPEAR
Opuntia erinacea
Cactus family (Cactaceae)

Description: Cactus plant, 4–12" tall and up to 3' wide. Large, flattened spatula- or egg-shaped pads are smooth and 2–8" long. Spines, ¼–4" long and 4–9 per cluster, are white, flattened at base, and straight or curved slightly downward. Flowers, 1½–3½" wide, are yellow, bronze, pink, or violet. Dry fruits are tan to brown and spiny.

Bloom Time: May to July.

Habitat/Range: Widespread in sandy or rocky soils in the Southwest.

Comments: When in bloom, these cacti form some of the most showy desert flowers. *Opuntia* is a Greek name for a spiny plant that grew near Opus, Greece. Common pricklypear may hybridize with several other species of *Opuntia*, making identification difficult. *O. polyacantha*, the plains pricklypear, is the other common *Opuntia* in the region.

YELLOW BEEPLANT
Cleome lutea
Caper family (Capparidaceae)

Description: Annual, 1–5' tall, with stout stems. Alternate leaves have 3–7 elliptical or lance-shaped leaflets, ⅜–2" long, arising from common point like fingers from the palm. Flowers have short stalk, 4 petals, and 6 to many stamens that protrude above top. Seed capsule, ⅜–1½" long, hangs downward on long stalk.

Bloom Time: April to August.

Habitat/Range: Sandy soils or disturbed areas in desert shrub and sagebrush communities up to 7,500', from eastern Washington to New Mexico and western Nebraska.

Comments: Some years, this annual will carpet large expanses with its yellow blooms. Flowers were boiled by Native Americans to make a black pigment for pottery paint. *Cleome* is an ancient Greek name for a different mustard plant.

FOURWING SALTBUSH
Atriplex canescens
Goosefoot family (Chenopodiaceae)

Description: Shrub averaging 2½–3' tall. Leaves, ⅜–1½" long, alternate and are linear to inversely lance-shaped, covered with small scales. Inconspicuous male and female flowers usually are found on separate plants. Yellow male flowers grow in tiny globular clusters; female flowers grow in open clusters that are 2–16" long. Flattened seeds have 4 large membranous wings.

Bloom Time: May to July.

Habitat/Range: Sandy soils in blackbrush, salt desert shrub, mountain brush, and pinyon-juniper communities from South Dakota to Texas.

Comments: Due to its drab flowers, the saltbush is easily overlooked. *Atriplex* is the Latin name for the plant, and *canescens* (grayish white) refers to the color of the leaves. In the past, the ground seeds were cooked as cereal, the leaves were cooked and eaten, and the ashes of the plant were used as a leavening for breads. Some Pueblo groups still use the plant. It's also a valuable browse plant for wildlife.

SHADSCALE
Atriplex confertifolia
Goosefoot family (Chenopodiaceae)

Description: Spiny shrub, 1–3' tall. Inconspicuous male and female flowers are on separate plants. Leaves alternate; blades are ⅜–¾" long, elliptical to oval, and covered with small scales on both sides. Yellow male flowers grow in small, tight clusters up to ⅜" long. Female flowers generally grow in leaf axils near branch tips. Fruit is a tiny seed.

Bloom Time: April to August.

Habitat/Range: Sandy to gravelly soils in salt desert shrub to pinyon-juniper communities from eastern Oregon to Texas.

Comments: Growing in saline soils, the leaves are edible but salty. *Confertifolia* (with flowers pressed together) refers to the tight floral clusters. A valuable forage plant for livestock, shadscale also hybridizes with several other *Atriplex* species.

COYOTE GOURD

Cucurbita foetidissima
Gourd family (Cucurbitaceae)

Description: Perennial vine with several stems that may reach up to 20' long. Large triangular leaves are shallowly lobed or angled along margins. Thick leaves are heart-shaped at base and pointed at tip. Funnel-shaped yellow flower, 3–5" long, has unpleasant scent. Fruit is a rounded gourd with stripes.

Bloom Time: June to August.

Habitat/Range: Disturbed sites and wash bottoms in blackbrush and pinyon-juniper woodlands from California east to Texas and Missouri.

Comments: *Cucurbita* is from a Latin word for a type of gourd. *Foetidissima* (fetid) refers to the strong odor of the crushed leaves, stems, or flowers. Another common name for the plant is stinking gourd. Ancestral Puebloans used the gourds for storage or water containers; seeds of the plant have been recovered in archaeological sites.

RUSSIAN-OLIVE

Elaeagnus angustifolia
Oleaster family (Elaeagnaceae)

Description: Small to moderately sized non-native tree, 15–36' high, with stout thorns along branches. Lance- to elliptically shaped leaves are narrow, 1–4½" long, and have silvery hairs that make leaves appear bicolored. Fragrant flowers, ½–1" long, have yellow lobes. Fruit is a seed encased in a mealy coating.

Bloom Time: May to August.

Habitat/Range: Riparian, marshy, or abandoned irrigation fields throughout the United States. Introduced and considered weedy.

Comments: *Elaeagnus* is from a Greek name for willows. *Angustifolia* (narrow-leaved) describes the leaves. Escaped from cultivation, the highly invasive Russian-olives spread into moist meadows and riparian areas, often forming dense thickets. The mealy fruits are edible and consumed by robins, gray foxes, raccoons, and other wildlife.

ROUNDLEAF BUFFALOBERRY
Shepherdia rotundifolia
Oleaster family (Elaeagnaceae)

Description: Evergreen shrub, 3–6' tall and 3–12' wide. Oval to egg- or lance-shaped leaves are ¼–1½" long, silvery green above, and pale-hairy below. Yellowish flowers grow in leaf axils and may be solitary or few to a cluster. Elliptical fruit has star-shaped hairs.

Bloom Time: May to July.

Habitat/Range: Mixed desert shrub, pinyon-juniper woodlands, and ponderosa pine communities up to 7,800' in the Southwest.

Comments: A distinct shrub endemic to the Colorado Plateau, it has odd-textured leaves that almost feel like Styrofoam. *Rotundifolia* refers to the rounded leaves. Westward settlers used the cooked berries to make a sauce for buffalo steaks; hence the common name. It's also called silverleaf due to the color of the leaves.

YELLOW MILKVETCH
Astragalus flavus
Pea family (Fabaceae)

Description: Perennial, 2–12" tall, growing erect or curved upward, and covered with star-shaped hairs. Compound leaves, 1⅛–6" long, have 9–21 linear to egg-shaped leaflets that are ¼–1" long. Leaves are smooth or with short, stiff hairs. Flower stalk bears 6–30 flowers; calyx tube is hairy and bell-shaped, and corolla is ¼–½" long and yellow. Seedpods, erect and oblong, up to ½" long, are covered with short, stiff hairs.

Bloom Time: May to June.

Habitat/Range: Saline soils in salt desert shrub communities at 3,830–5,400'.

Comments: *Flavus* (yellow) refers to the flower color. Plants are toxic to livestock. Several varieties exist and may have pink-purple to white flowers. Blooming plants often cover large patches of ground.

YELLOW SWEET-CLOVER
Melilotus officinalis
Pea family (Fabaceae)

Description: Annual or biennial, with stems 2–5'
or more and covered with stiff hairs pressed close
to surface. Compound leaves have short petioles;
3 leaflets are wedge-shaped or elliptical, ¼–1½"
long, and with toothed margins. Flower stalk bears
20–65 yellow flowers that are about ¼" long.
Seedpods contain 1–2 seeds and are ⅛" long.

Bloom Time: May to September.

Habitat/Range: Introduced from Europe and now
widespread in North America.

Comments: *Melilotus* (honey plant) refers to the
plant's use in the honey industry. *Officinalis* means
that it was officially sold as an herb or used in
medicine. Sweet-clover was used in teas to treat
intestinal worms or earaches or as a poultice for
swollen joints.

GOLDEN PEA
Thermopsis montana
Pea family (Fabaceae)

Description: Perennial. Stems 1–3' tall, clustered, and may be covered with fine hairs. Leaves are compound; 3 leaflets are ¾–3½" long, elliptical to lance-shaped, and pointed or rounded at tip. Flower stalk has 2–23 pea-shaped yellow flowers, ¾–1⅛" long. Slightly hairy pods turn black at maturity.

Bloom Time: May to July.

Habitat/Range: Moist sites in pinyon-juniper, riparian, and ponderosa pine communities, 3,900–10,500', from British Columbia to New Mexico.

Comments: *Thermopsis* is from the Greek *thermos* (lupine) and *opsis* (resemblance), referring to the plant's likeness to the lupines. *Montana* (mountain) refers to the plant's higher-elevation distribution. Sometimes, though, it's found growing in canyon bottoms.

GOLDEN CORYDALIS
Corydalis aurea
Fumitory family (Furmariaceae)

Description: Annual or biennial, 2½–15" tall, and clump-forming. Leaves are compound; linear to oblong leaflets are several times divided. Flower stem bears few to many yellowish flowers, ½–¾" long, with 4 petals. Outer pair of petals is generally hooded above; 1 petal is spur-shaped at base.

Bloom Time: June to September.

Habitat/Range: Warm desert shrub to pinyon-juniper woodlands and up to alpine areas in moist sites.

Comments: *Corydalis* (crested lark) refers to the spur-shaped petal, which resembles the claw of a lark. *Aurea* (golden) refers to the flower color. It's sometimes planted in urban gardens.

BEAUTIFUL BLAZINGSTAR
Mentzelia laevicaulis
Stickleaf family (Loasaceae)

Description: Perennial or biennial growing up to 3' tall. White stems form many branches. Basal leaves are lance-shaped, up to 4" long, toothed along margins, and have rough texture. Upper leaves are smaller. Starlike flower, 3" wide, has 5 pointed petals and short, green bract between petals. Numerous threadlike stamens project above flower. Fruit is a woody capsule with numerous tiny black seeds.

Bloom Time: June to August.

Habitat/Range: Dry sandy or gravelly soils, sometimes on steep slopes, in salt desert shrub, mountain brush, and pinyon-juniper communities from Washington to Montana and south to California and Nevada.

Comments: *Mentzelia* honors Christian Mentzel (1622–1701), a German botanist and physician. *Laevicaulis* (smooth stem) describes the texture of the stems. Night blooming, the flowers open in late afternoon and close in the morning and are pollinated by moths and other night-flying insects.

DESERT STICKLEAF
Mentzelia multiflora
Stickleaf family (Loasaceae)

Description: Stout-stemmed perennial, 1–3' tall. Upper portions of stem and leaves have rough, coarse hairs. Lower leaves are lance-shaped, ¾–2¼", with lobes halfway to midrib, rounded or toothed. Leaves are sticky; sand often sticks to their surfaces. Upper leaves are smaller. Yellowish flowers are borne in small clusters; flowers, ½–¼" wide, have 5 outer petals longer and wider than inner ones. Fruit is an urn-shaped capsule.

Bloom Time: May to August.

Habitat/Range: Sandy soils in salt desert shrub to sagebrush communities at 3,900–5,700', from the Southwest to California and north to Wyoming.

Comments: *Mentzelia* honors Christian Mentzel (1622–1701), a German botanist. *Multiflora* (many flowers) refers to the quantity of flowers, which open in the afternoon.

LAVENDER-LEAF SUNDROPS
Calyophus lavandulifolia
Evening Primrose family (Onagraceae)

Description: Low-growing perennial, ¾–9" tall. Leaves, ¼–1½" long and linear to inversely lance-shaped, are covered with dense hairs and have wedge-shaped bases. Solitary yellow flowers grow in leaf axils; corolla tube is ¾–3" long, and 4 flaring petals have ruffled edges.

Bloom Time: May to July.

Habitat/Range: Blackbrush and mixed desert shrub up to pinyon-juniper and ponderosa pine communities to 8,500' in the Southwest and north to South Dakota.

Comments: Striking yellow flowers fade to shades of orange or lavender upon drying; hence the common name. *Calyophus* is from the Greek *caly* (calyx) and *lophus* (a crest), referring to the small projection on the sepals. *Lavandulifolia* (lavender-like leaves) refers to the resemblance of the leaves to those of lavender.

BRIDGES EVENING PRIMROSE
Oenothera longissima
Evening Primrose family (Onagraceae)

Description: Biennial or perennial, with stems 3–6' or taller. Elliptical or lance- or inversely lance-shaped leaves are ¾–10" long with entire or wavy-toothed edges. Solitary yellow flowers up to 4½" long, with long tube, are borne in upper leaf axils. Upright capsules split at maturity and release numerous tiny black seeds.

Bloom Time: June to October.

Habitat/Range: Sand or gravel along stream banks and riparian communities, 2,525–7,200' in southeastern Utah.

Comments: The type specimen is from Natural Bridges National Monument; hence the common name. *Longissima* refers to the long corolla tube. *O. elata*, Hooker's evening primrose, is similar but with a shorter corolla tube.

WINGED BUCKWHEAT
Eriogonum alatum
Buckwheat family (Polygonaceae)

Description: Perennial, mainly 1–4' tall. Stout stem arises from a basal cluster of leaves, which are often withered but still attached at maturity. Lance- or inversely lance-shaped leaves, 1⅛–5" long, are covered with stiff, short hairs. Stem leaves are smaller and fewer upward. Flowers lack petals; petal-like sepals are yellowish to greenish and borne in clusters. Seeds are ¼" long and have 3 wings.

Bloom Time: June to September.

Habitat/Range: Sandy soils in mixed desert shrub to mountain brush communities from Wyoming to Mexico.

Comments: *Eriogonum* (woolly knee) refers to hairs located at the swollen stem joints of many species in this genus. *Alatum* (winged) refers to the seeds' wings, which aid in seed dispersal by the wind.

DESERT TRUMPET
Eriogonum inflatum
Buckwheat family (Polygonaceae)

Description: Annual or perennial, mostly 1–3' tall. Smooth, greenish or brownish hollow stems are inflated near joints. Basal leaves are long-stalked; blades rounded and up to 1⅛" wide with wavy margins. Many-branched flowering stalks arise from a common point; minute, yellowish or reddish petal-less flowers are borne along slender branches. Fruit is a seed.

Bloom Time: April to August.

Habitat/Range: Wide range of soil types from salt desert shrub to pinyon-juniper communities.

Comments: *Inflatum* (inflated) refers to the shape of the stem. Native Americans ate the young stems raw or cooked. The unique swollen stems easily identify the desert trumpets, and these stems may persist through the winter.

SULFUR-FLOWERED BUCKWHEAT
Eriogonum umbellatum
Buckwheat family (Polygonaceae)

Description: Perennial that has basal mat of egg- to spoon-shaped leaves, green above and gray-woolly below. Mats may be 5–50" wide. Arising from basal leaves are flowering stems 2–20" tall that bear clusters of numerous small, yellowish flowers. Individual flowers have 6 lobes and stamens that extend beyond flower opening and may have pinkish tinge. Fruit is a 3-angled seed.

Bloom Time: May to September.

Habitat/Range: Dry, rocky sites in sagebrush to aspen communities across the West.

Comments: *Eriogonum* (woolly knees) refers to the hairy, swollen joints of many buckwheat species. *Umbellatum* (umbrella-like) refers to the arrangement of the flowers in an umbel. The common name indicates the color of the flowers.

SAGEBRUSH BUTTERCUP
Ranunculus glaberrimus
Buttercup family (Ranuculaceae)

Description: Low-growing perennial, 2–6" tall, that arises from clustered roots. Basal leaves are fleshy and either broad with shallow lobes or divided into deeper lobes. Short flowering stem bears bright yellow flower, 1" wide. Flower has 4–7 petals and numerous stamens and pistils; petals have nectar gland at their base. Fruit is a seed.

Bloom Time: March to June.

Habitat/Range: Seasonally moist sites in sagebrush to aspen communities up to 9,500', from British Columbia to the Four Corners region.

Comments: *Glaberrimus* (without hairs) refers to the smooth leaves. Insect pollinators such as beetles, flies, wasps, and others are attracted to these flowers.

BUR BUTTERCUP

Ranunculus testiculatus
Buttercup family (Ranunculaceae)

Description: Annual, with hairy stems trailing along ground. Basal leaves are deeply 3-parted, the segments again lobed into linear parts. Sepals, 4, are green and hairy; yellow petals, 2–5, are ¼–½" long and hairy. Seeds are hairy.

Bloom Time: March to July.

Habitat/Range: Widely distributed in rangelands across the West; does well in disturbed sites. Introduced from Eurasia.

Comments: *Ranunculus* (small frog) refers to many of the plants in this genus that grow in moist locations. Presence of bur buttercup indicates problems with rangeland health.

BLACKBRUSH

Coleogyne ramosissima
Rose family (Rosaceae)

Description: Rounded shrub up to 4' tall, with dense branches that may be spiny at tip. Narrow, inversely lance-shaped leaves arranged oppositely are evergreen, up to ⅜" long, and with small point at tip. Flowers, about ½" across, have many stamens; may lack petals entirely or have up to 4. Yellowish sepals, 4, are brownish beneath; woody sepals may persist. Fruit is a small egg-shaped seed.

Bloom Time: April to July.

Habitat/Range: Shallow soil in blackbrush to warm desert shrub communities up to 5,700', from California to Colorado.

Comments: Blackbrush form vast plant communities throughout the Canyonlands region. *Ramosissima* (many branched) refers to the intricate branching habit of the shrub. Branches darken when wet; hence the common name.

LARGE-LEAVED AVENS
Geum macrophyllum
Rose family (Rosaceae)

Description: Large perennial that grows up to 3' tall. Basal leaves have rough hairs and are irregularly divided into small leaflets with larger heart- to kidney-shaped leaflet at tip. Stem leaves have 3 deep lobes or divisions. Saucer-shaped yellow flowers, ½" wide, have 5 rounded petals surrounding center of numerous yellow stamens. Fruit is a seed with hooked bristles.

Bloom Time: May to August.

Habitat/Range: Open forests and edges in ponderosa pine and higher-elevation forests, 4,000–9,500', across much of North America.

Comments: *Geum* is the Latin name for this plant. *Macrophyllum* (large-leaved) refers to the large basal leaves. Native Americans used this plant medicinally for eyewashes, stomach ailments, and child birthing relief. The hooked bristles on the seeds attach themselves to the fur of animals that come in contact with the fruits to aid in dispersal.

ANTELOPE BITTERBRUSH
Purshia tridentata
Rose family (Rosaceae)

Description: Scraggly-looking shrub that grows 1–6' tall. Wedge-shaped leaves are ½–1" long, hairy below, and 3-lobed at the tip. Numerous yellow flowers have 5 petals, numerous stamens, and are ½–1" wide. Fruit is a seed.

Bloom Time: May to August.

Habitat/Range: Drier sites in sagebrush, pinyon-juniper, and ponderosa pine communities from British Columbia to Colorado.

Comments: *Purshia* honors Frederick Traugott Pursh (1774–1820), a German botanist who worked on the Lewis and Clark expedition plant collection and wrote a guide to North American plants, *Flora Americae Septentrionalis*, in 1814. *Tridentata* (three-toothed) refers to the lobes at the leaf tips. Bitterbrush is an important browse plant for wildlife.

GOLDEN CURRANT

Ribes aureum
Saxifrage family (Saxifragaceae)

Description: Shrub, 3–9' tall, with smooth, thornless branchlets. Leaf blades are rounded to kidney-shaped, ⅜–3" wide, and 3-lobed; the lobes again lobed or toothed. Yellow sepals, 5, are petal-like; petals are smaller and yellow or reddish. Berries are smooth, black, red, orange, or translucent golden.

Bloom Time: April to July.

Habitat/Range: Riparian, sagebrush, pinyon-juniper, and higher-elevation plant communities from the Pacific Northwest to New Mexico.

Comments: *Ribes* is from the Arabic *ribas* (acid-tasting), in reference to the edible but tart fruit. These plants grow near springs, hanging gardens, or other moist sites.

YELLOW MONKEYFLOWER

Mimulus guttatus
Figwort family (Scrophulariaceae)

Description: Seemingly delicate perennial arising on stems 2–50" tall. Broad oval leaves are arranged oppositely along stems and are toothed along margins. Yellow flowers, ½–1½" long, are tubular in outline with petals flaring at opening. Calyx that subtends flower becomes inflated when fruits form. Fruit is a thin-walled capsule.

Bloom Time: May to July.

Habitat/Range: Moist sites in seeps, hanging gardens, and marshy areas, 2,650–9,820', across much of western North America.

Comments: *Mimulus* (mimic) refers to the flower resembling a monkey's face and the habit of clinging to a wall like a monkey. *Guttatus* (spotted) refers to the red spots on the flower's lower lip. These spots act as nectar guides directing pollinators into the flower.

PINK AND PURPLE FLOWERS

This section includes flowers ranging from pink to purple and shades in between. Some bluish plants may be in this section, but be sure to also check the blue flower section.

SHOWY MILKWEED

Asclepias speciosa
Milkweed family (Asclepiadaceae)

Description: Stout perennial, 3–6' tall, with unbranched stems containing milky sap. Stem and undersides of leaves may be covered with dense white hairs. Oval leaves, arranged oppositely, are 1–6" across and 2¼–8" long. Flowers in rounded clusters hang from short stout stalks. Flowers are over 1" wide and have 5 rose-purple petals and 5 pinkish-cream needle-like, pouch-shaped hoods. Pods are 3–5" long, spiny or smooth.

Bloom Time: May to September.

Habitat/Range: Disturbed sites, riparian areas, or moist locations throughout the West.

Comments: Monarch butterfly larvae consume the toxic foliage of this plant, which makes this insect less palatable to predators. The silky down of the seedpods, which is 5 or 6 times more buoyant than cork, was used to stuff pillows and World War II–era life jackets and flight suits. *Speciosa* means this is the common species of the genus.

RUSSIAN KNAPWEED

Centaurea repens
Sunflower family (Asteraceae)

Description: Perennial noxious weed with smooth stem, 1–3' tall, bearing cobwebby hairs. Basal leaves wither when flowers bloom; narrow stem leaves, ⅜–2½" long, may be toothed along margins. Outer bracts beneath flower heads are broad. Flower heads, ⅜–1" wide and urn-shaped, have disk flowers that are tubular and pink or purplish.

Bloom Time: May to August.

Habitat/Range: Disturbed locations, often seasonally moist, throughout North America.

Comments: Noxious weed introduced from Eurasia is now widely established in North America. *Centaurea* refers to the centaur, Chiron. *Repens* (creeping) refers to the plant's habit of spreading by underground roots.

RYDBERG'S THISTLE
Cirsium rydbergii
Sunflower family (Asteraceae)

Description: Herbaceous perennial. Lower part of stem is covered with brown leaf bases. Huge basal leaves, 1–3' long and 6–18" wide, are doubly lobed; lobes are narrow or wide. Spines along leaf edges are up to ⅜" long. Stems, 2–4' tall, have smooth leaves that are smaller upward. Flower heads are ⅜–¾" high and ⅜–1⅛" wide. Outer bracts below heads abruptly end in downward curved spines. Flowers are pink.

Bloom Time: May to August.

Habitat/Range: Hanging gardens or canyons, 3,500–4,750', in southeastern Utah.

Comments: The huge basal rosettes, tall flowering stems, and small heads make this thistle relatively easy to identify. *Rydbergii* honors Per Axel Rydberg (1860–1931), an American botanist who was an authority on Western plants. Hummingbirds, moths, and butterflies pollinate these flowers.

SHOWY RUSHPINK
Lygodesmia grandiflora
Sunflower family (Asteraceae)

Description: Perennial, with stems 2–20" tall and slender branches. Leaves are alternate, ¼–4" long, and mostly linear to lance-shaped. Flower heads are cylindrical with 5–10 pink or pinkish-purple to lavender-blue ray flowers that are ¾–1½" long. Pappus has finely barbed bristles.

Bloom Time: May to July.

Habitat/Range: Mixed desert shrub, grasslands, sagebrush, and pinyon-juniper communities in southeastern Utah and into Arizona.

Comments: *Lygodesmia* is from the Greek *lygos* (pliant) and *desmia* (bundle), in reference to the clustered stems, which are very pliant and twig-like. *Grandiflora* (large flowers) refers to the size of the showy flowers.

TANSYLEAF ASTER
Machaeranthera tanacetifolia
Sunflower family (Asteraceae)

Description: Herbaceous annual, 3–20" tall, and with glandular or long, soft hairs. Leaves, ⅜–2½" long, are highly dissected to midrib, with each segment ending in a small, spiny bristle. Flower heads are ⅜" high and ⅜–¾" wide, with bracts lance-shaped to linear. Ray flowers, 11–23 pink-purple or blue-purple, surround central cluster of yellow disk flowers.

Bloom Time: June to October.

Habitat/Range: Blackbrush, mixed desert shrub, and pinyon-juniper communities in southern Utah.

Comments: *Machaeranthera* (sickle anther) refers to the shape of the anthers. *Tanacetifolia* (tansy-like leaves) refers to the fernlike leaves, which make this an easy aster to identify. Two other common *Machaeranthera* are *M. canescens*, hoary aster, and *M. bigelowii*, Bigelow's aster.

113

ANNUAL WIRELETTUCE
Stephanomeria exigua
Sunflower family (Asteraceae)

Description: Annual or biennial, with herbage smooth or covered with fine hairs. Slender, wiry stems grow erect, 2–24" tall. Main leaves are deeply divided to midline, with lobes sometimes divided again. Upper leaves are few and smaller. Flower heads, ½" wide, have pink to white ray flowers only; rays are toothed at their tips.

Bloom Time: April to September.

Habitat/Range: Warm desert shrub to pinyon-juniper communities from Oregon to New Mexico.

Comments: *Stephanomeria* (crown divided) refers to the spaces between the ray flowers. *Exigua* refers to the milky latex that is exuded from the plant. This plant is a relative of cultivated lettuce, and its bitter leaves may be eaten.

DESERT ROCKCRESS
Arabis pulchra
Mustard family (Brassicaceae)

Description: Perennial, to 2' tall. Stems have fine, branching hairs throughout or are smooth above. Basal leaves are arranged in poorly developed rosettes; leaves are ⅜–2⅜" long, narrow, and inversely lance- or spatula-shaped. Flowers, ½" wide, have 4 pale pink to white petals. Thin pods, up to 2½" long, curve downward at maturity.

Bloom Time: April to July.

Habitat/Range: Mixed desert shrub and pinyon-juniper communities in the Four Corners region.

Comments: *Arabis* (from Arabia) denotes where a member of this genus was first described. Desert rockcress is often found growing from cracks in slickrock. Pretty rockcress, *A. perennans*, has smaller purple flowers.

RAVEN TENNYSON

AFRICAN MUSTARD
Malcolmia africana
Mustard family (Brassicaceae)

Description: Annual weed, with stems 1–16" tall or low growing and covered with forked or 3-rayed hairs. Leaves are mainly basal, ½–3½" long, inversely lance-shaped or elliptical, and toothed along margins. Flowers, ¼–½" wide, have 4 pink to lavender petals and 4 reddish-purple sepals. Seedpods are straight and 1–3" long.

Bloom Time: April to July.

Habitat/Range: Throughout the western United States.

Comments: *Malcolmia* is for William Malcolm (1778–1805), a British horticulturist. *Africana* is for this exotic weed's home continent: Africa. At times, large fields may be covered with these plants.

WHIPPLE'S FISHHOOK
Sclerocactus whipplei
Cactus family (Cactaceae)

Description: Solitary or occasionally small colonies of cylindrical or circular plants. Stems are mostly 2–14" tall and up to 6" in diameter. Main spines are ⅜–3" long; most are hooked at the tip like a fishhook. Flowers are mainly pink, white, or yellow and up to 2" long.

Bloom Time: April to July.

Habitat/Range: Salt and mixed desert shrub up to pinyon-juniper communities in the Southwest.

Comments: These small barrel-shaped cacti have beautiful flowers and fishhook-shaped spines. *Whipplei* honors Amiel Wicks Whipple (1818–1863), a topographical engineer who served on a boundary survey between the United States and Mexico in 1853–1856 and was the leader of the Pacific Railroad Survey on the 35th Parallel. Some specimens may have straight spines and/or variously colored flowers.

ROCKY MOUNTAIN BEEPLANT
Cleome serrulata
Caper family (Capparidaceae)

Description: Annual that grows 1–6' or more tall and may have numerous branches. Compound leaves are smooth to slightly hairy and have 3 lance-shaped to elliptical leaflets that are ¾–3½" long. Flowering stalks bear ½"-long pink to reddish-purple flowers (sometimes white) that have 4 petals and 6 stamens. Slender seed pods are about 2" long and bear rounded, rough-textured seeds.

Bloom Time: June to September.

Habitat/Range: Disturbed sites from Washington to the Southwest and east into the Great Plains.

Comments: The flowers produce great quantities of nectar that attract bees; thus, the common name. Native Americans ate the cooked leaves and created black pottery paint from boiled plants. *Serrulata* (finely saw-toothed) refers to the leaf edges.

LONG-FLOWER SNOWBERRY
Symphoricarpos longiflorus
Honeysuckle family (Caprifoliaceae)

Description: Woody shrub to 3' tall. Young stems are either smooth or covered with fine, soft hairs. Opposite leaves are oval or lance-shaped and ½" long. Flowers, solitary or in pairs, grow in the angle between leaf and stem, often hanging downward. Slender corolla tube, ¼–¾" long, is blue to deep pink and flares open at mouth. Fruit is a white 2-seeded berry.

Bloom Time: May to July.

Habitat/Range: Pinyon-juniper up to ponderosa pine and hanging gardens from California to Mexico across the Southwest.

Comments: *Symphoricarpos* is from the Greek *syn* (together), *phorein* (to bear), and *karpos* (fruit), referring to the closely clustered, snow-white fruits. *Longiflorus* (long flower) refers to the flower shape. *S. oreophilus,* mountain snowberry, occurs at higher elevations.

GREASEWOOD
Sarcobatus vermiculatus
Goosefoot family (Chenopodiaceae)

Description: Thorny shrub, 3–7' tall, with white bark and linear succulent leaves, ¼–1¾" long. Male and female flowers are separate but found on same plant. Rose male flowers are arranged spirally along short, often upright spike; female flowers are fewer but also arranged along a short spike in axils of leaves. Seeds are cup-shaped below a papery wing.

Bloom Time: April to August.

Habitat/Range: Saline soils in salt desert shrub communities from eastern Washington to Texas.

Comments: Greasewood grows in alkaline soils; sodium or potassium salts often accumulate in or on the leaves. *Sarcobatus* is from the Greek *sarco* (flesh) and *batos* (bramble), referring to the succulent leaves and spiny branches. The tough wood was used for tools or firewood.

CRESCENT MILKVETCH
Astragalus amphioxys
Pea family (Fabaceae)

Description: Low-growing, early-season perennial. Compound leaves up to 1½" long have 5–21 elliptical or egg-shaped leaflets per leaf. Leaves and stems are covered with soft grayish hairs. Leafless flowering stalks, ¾–8" tall, bear 2–13 flowers near the tip. Purplish-pink flowers, ½–1" long, have tubular calyx and upper 2 petals fused together, forming a hood. Lower 3 petals are small and overlapping. Crescent-shaped pods are smooth, compressed at both ends, and 1½" long.

Bloom Time: March to June.

Habitat/Range: Salt and cold desert shrub, blackbrush, and pinyon-juniper communities, 2,090–6,240' in the Southwest.

Comments: Crescent milkvetch, named for the shape of the seedpods, blooms early in the spring. *Amphioxys* comes from *amphi* (on both ends) and *oxys* (sharp), which refers to the compressed ends on the seedpods.

PAINTED MILKVETCH
Astragalus ceramicus
Pea family (Fabaceae)

Description: Perennial, with stems sprawling to erect, 1–16" long, and covered with pickaxe-shaped hairs. Leaves are compound and ¾–6" long; 3–13 leaflets are ¼–1" long and thread-like. Flower stalks have 2–15 dull purple or pink flowers, ¼–½" long. Distinctive pods are inflated, elliptical, and have reddish mottling.

Bloom Time: April to June.

Habitat/Range: Sandy soils in mixed desert shrub, grasslands, and pinyon-juniper communities from Idaho to New Mexico and Oklahoma.

Comments: Painted milkvetch grows in sandy locations. *Ceramicus* refers to the pod's pottery-like appearance. Easily overlooked due to their low-growing habit, the inflated seedpods are beautiful.

RIMROCK MILKVETCH
Astragalus desperatus
Pea family (Fabaceae)

Description: Low-growing perennial, ½–4½" tall. Compound leaves, ½–4½" long, have 7–17 ellipti-cal or inversely lance-shaped leaflets. Main flower stalk grows up to 5" tall; individual flowers arise on short stems. Calyx tube may be ½" long and bell-shaped; pink-purple or two-toned petals are ¼" long. Seedpods are elliptical or curved, up to ¾" long, and covered with stiff hairs.

Bloom Time: March to August.

Habitat/Range: Mixed desert shrub and pinyon-juniper communities on the Colorado Plateau.

Comments: *Astragalus* is the Greek name for legume, which may be derived from *astragalos* (ankle bone), in reference to the shape of the leaves or pods. The rimrock milkvetch is a Colorado Plateau endemic.

WOOLLY LOCOWEED

Astragalus mollissimus
Pea family (Fabaceae)

Description: Perennial that grows from very short stem or none at all, 2–34" tall. Compound leaves, ¾–11" long, have 15–35 woolly elliptical to egg-shaped leaflets. Flower stalks, ¾–10" long, are purplish and densely covered with hairs. Flowers 7–20 per stalk; calyx is ¼–½" long, hairy, and with 5 pointed teeth. Flowers, ¾" long, are pink-purple or bicolored with some white; upper petal flares at end. Egg-shaped seedpods, ⅓–1" long, are densely hairy.

Bloom Time: March to August.

Habitat/Range: Grassland to pinyon-juniper communities, 3,525–7,270', from Wyoming to Mexico.

Comments: *Mollissimus* (most soft) refers to the dense hairy covering of the leaves and stems, which also inspires the common name. Plants contain an alkaloid, locoine, which can cause livestock to "go loco," or even die, if they eat too much of this species.

PREUSS' MILKVETCH

Astragalus preussii
Pea family (Fabaceae)

Description: Perennial or annual, stems 4–15" long, reddish, and growing upright from woody base. Compound leaves are 1½–5" long; 7–25 elliptical to rounded smooth leaflets are ¾" long. Flowers 3–22 per stalk; small, green, 5-toothed calyx subtends tubular set of petals. Upper petal is large and flares at tip. Flowers are pinkish-purple, white, or bicolored and about ¾" long. Pods are elliptical, smooth or covered with soft hairs, ¾" long, and become papery or leathery upon drying.

Bloom Time: March to June.

Habitat/Range: Selenium-rich soils in salt desert shrub and pinyon-juniper communities in the Southwest. May grow in profusion along roadsides.

Comments: Preuss' milkvetch prefers selenium-bearing soils and may be toxic to livestock. The plant is named for Charles Preuss (1803–1854), a talented scientist and cartographer who joined three of John C. Frémont's Western expeditions.

NORTHERN SWEETVETCH
Hedysarum boreale
Pea family (Fabaceae)

Description: Perennial with bunched stems up to 35" tall. Compound leaves are 1½–6" long with 5–15 elliptical to lance-shaped leaflets. Leaflets may or may not be hairy. Flowering stalks bear numerous pink to purple-pink flowers that are ½–1" long; keel petal is longer than other lower 2. Fruit is a pod with 2–8 rounded segments.

Bloom Time: May to September.

Habitat/Range: Mixed desert shrub up to aspen communities from Alberta to Texas.

Comments: *Hedysarum* (sweet) refers to the fragrant flowers. *Boreale* (northern) indicates the northern range of this species. The flattened seedpods are distinct.

LAMBERT'S LOCOWEED
Oxytropis lambertii
Pea family (Fabaceae)

Description: Colorful perennial with hairy stems that grows 7–25" tall. Compound leaves are 1½–12" long and bear 7–13 lance-shaped to linear leaflets. Upright flowering stems bear dense clusters of reddish-lavender to purple pea-shaped flowers. Individual flowers are ½–1" long and tube-shaped. Fruit is a cylindrical to lance-shaped pod, pointed at the tip.

Bloom Time: May to August.

Habitat/Range: Mixed desert shrub, grasslands, and pinyon-juniper communities from the Southwest north to Canada.

Comments: This plant is toxic to all livestock. *Oxytropis* (sharp keel) refers to the pointed tip formed by the 2 lower petals or keel. *Lambertii* honors Aylmer Bourke Lambert (1761–1842), an English botanist.

HERONSBILL
Erodium cicutarium
Geranium family (Geraniaceae)

Description: Weedy annual that grows in wild or cultivated areas. Stems are low growing or prostrate, usually 2–5" long, and covered with small, stiff hairs that are sticky. Leaves are up to 4½" long and fernlike; each deeply divided leaflet is irregularly lobed or toothed. Bright pink flowers, ¼–½" across, are borne in small clusters. Elongated fruit tapers like a bird's beak.

Bloom Time: March to September.

Habitat/Range: Disturbed sites throughout the western United States.

Comments: Introduced from the Mediterranean region, this plant was noted in Utah in 1844 by John C. Frémont. The auger-shaped seeds "burrow" into the soil with the help of the long seed tail. *Erodium* is from the Greek *erodios* (heron), referring to the shape of the fruit; *cicutarium* (like *Cicuta*) refers to the resemblance of the leaves to water-hemlock, *Cicuta maculata*.

SCORPIONWEED
Phacelia crenulata
Waterleaf family (Hydrophyllaceae)

Description: Annual, 2–32" tall, that may grow in profusion. Basal leaves are strap-shaped to elliptical, with margins deeply lobed or wavy. Sticky, glandular hairs mix with nonglandular hairs along leaves and stems. Flowers grow along elongated axis that curls like a scorpion's tail. Blue-violet to purple flowers are ¼" long and bell-shaped; stamens and style protrude above flowers.

Bloom Time: April to July.

Habitat/Range: Salt and cool desert shrub, pinyon-juniper, and mountain brush communities in the Southwest.

Comments: *Phacelia* is from the Greek *phakelos* (fascicle), referring to the clustered flowers. *Crenulata* (shallow, rounded teeth) refers to the leaf margin. Foliage is strong smelling.

PURPLE SAGE
Poliomintha incana
Mint family (Lamiaceae)

Description: Woody shrub, 12–40" tall, with rounded or square stems. Opposite linear leaves are ⅜–1⅛" long and are covered with dense white hairs. Flowers are borne in upper leaf axils; corolla is 2-lipped, ½" long, and lavender to whitish with purple dots on lower lip.

Bloom Time: April to August.

Habitat/Range: Mixed desert shrub and pinyon-juniper communities, often in sandy sites from California to Texas.

Comments: These wispy-looking shrubs grow in sand dunes. *Poliomintha* (gray mint) is a reference to the plant's dense hairs, which give it a gray appearance. The flowers are used as a seasoning. The calyx has a purplish cast that gives the plant its common name.

PRAIRIE WILD ONION
Allium textile
Lily family (Liliaceae)

Description: Perennial, with buried ¾"-thick bulb. Threadlike leaves, 2–4 per flowering stalk, can be up to 9" long. Leafless flowering stalk, 1–9" long, bears round cluster of 5–54 flowers; 3 sepals and 3 petals are white or pale pink with deep purple nectar guides. Fruit is a small capsule.

Bloom Time: April to July.

Habitat/Range: Salt desert shrub, sagebrush, and pinyon-juniper communities up to 7,150', from Canada south to New Mexico.

Comments: *Allium* (to avoid) refers to the odor and flavor of the edible bulbs. *Textile* (textile or fabric) refers to the dark brown fabric-like fibers that loosely encase the bulb.

PURPLE LOOSESTRIFE
Lythrum salicaria
Loosestrife family (Lythraceae)

Description: Annual or perennial with 4-angled stems that may reach 4–5' tall or more. Variable leaves are 1–5" long and lance-shaped. Leaf bases are rounded or heart-shaped. Purplish flowers are borne in dense clusters; there are 10–14 stamens per flower. Fruit is a club-shaped capsule.

Bloom Time: July to September.

Habitat/Range: Wetlands and marshy areas throughout the United States. Considered a noxious weed, the species is native to Europe.

Comments: *Lythrum* (blood) refers to the color of the flowers. *Salicaria* (willow-like) refers to the stature of the plant. These plants may spread in wetlands if left unchecked, but are often targeted for eradication.

TRAILING FOUR O'CLOCK
Allionia incarnata
Four O'Clock family (Nyctaginaceae)

Description: Perennial, with stems growing along ground, 4–36" long, radiating from central root crown. Leaves and stems have sticky hairs. Leaves are opposite but unequal in length, ⅜–1⅛" long, and egg-shaped to elliptical. Magenta to pink-purple flowers are ¼–¾" long and lack true petals.

Bloom Time: May to October.

Habitat/Range: Blackbrush, salt desert shrub, and pinyon-juniper communities from southern California to Utah and Colorado and south into Mexico and South America.

Comments: Flowers open in the afternoon; hence the common name. However, the flowers remain open most of the day.

SHOWY FOUR O'CLOCK
Mirabilis multiflora
Four O'Clock family (Nyctaginaceae)

Description: Perennial clump-forming plant, mainly 1–3' tall and as broad or broader. Opposite, short-petioled leaves are rounded to egg-shaped, ¾–7" long, and may be pointed at tip. Flowers grow in small clusters in leaf axils; individual magenta flowers are 1½–2¼" long and funnel-shaped.

Bloom Time: May to August.

Habitat/Range: Blackbrush and pinyon-juniper communities, 2,370–7,425', throughout the Southwest.

Comments: When in bloom, these are among the most beautiful flowers in Canyon Country. *Mirabilis* (marvelous) and *multiflora* (many-flowered) describe this beautiful plant. The flowers open in the late afternoon—not necessarily at four o'clock sharp, however. Pollination may be by night-flying insects and moths.

FIREWEED
Epilobium angustifolium
Evening Primrose family (Onagraceae)

Description: Perennial arising on stems 2–9' tall, mostly unbranched. Stalkless leaves are lance-shaped and 2–10" long. Elongated clusters of flowers arise at ends of flowering stems. Rose to reddish-purple flowers are 1–2" wide and have 4 petals and 4-lobed stigma. Long podlike capsule splits open to release numerous white-haired seeds.

Bloom Time: June to October.

Habitat/Range: Burned forests, disturbed sites, meadows, or along roadsides, 4,750–11,300', across much of North America.

Comments: *Augustifolium* (having narrow leaves) refers to the lance-shaped leaves. The common name refers to the plant's habit of colonizing recently burned areas; fireweed was one of the first plants to sprout from the burned areas after the 1980 Mount Saint Helens eruption. The upright spikes of flowers attract bees as pollinators.

CLUSTERED CANCERROOT
Orobanche fasiculata
Broomrape family (Orobanchaceae)

Description: Small, parasitic plant with clustered stems that arise up to 8". Fleshy stems are purplish or yellowish and often branch underground. Scalelike leaves are small and non-green. Tubular flowers are borne on ends of flowering stalks and have a cup-shaped calyx with triangular lobes. Curved floral tube is purple, yellow, or brownish, flares open at the end, and is ¾–2" long.

Bloom Time: May to August.

Habitat/Range: Sandy sites in warm desert shrub up to fir communities 3,830–10,175', across much of the western United States and the Yukon Territory.

Comments: *Orobanche* is from *orobos* (clinging plant) and *ancho* (to strangle), which refers to its parasitic nature. *Fasiculata* (clustered) refers to the multiple stems. This plant has a variety of hosts, but mainly parasitizes *Artemisia* species.

CAVE PRIMROSE
Primula specuicola
Primrose family (Primulaceae)

Description: Perennial, 2–11" long, with withered leaves at base. Leaves, ¾–8" long, are spatula-shaped to elliptical, variously toothed along margins, and white-mealy below, greener above. Lavender to pink flowers with corolla tube rimmed in yellow are ½–⅔" wide and grow in clusters at end of leafless stalk.

Bloom Time: February to June.

Habitat/Range: Seeps and hanging gardens on the Colorado Plateau.

Comments: A Colorado Plateau endemic, this spectacular wildflower blooms around Easter; another common name is Easter flower. *Primula* is a diminutive of *primus* (first), another reference to the plant's bloom time in early spring.

VASE FLOWER
Clematis hirsutissima
Buttercup family (Ranunculaceae)

Description: Perennial, stems 10–35" long and often bearing long hairs. Compound leaves have 2–6 pairs, and leaflets may be divided several times into narrow segments. Solitary flowers are brownish purple and have 4 sepals but no petals. Urn-shaped flowers often hang downward on curved stalks. Seeds have long, hairy plumes at maturity.

Bloom Time: May to August.

Habitat/Range: Sagebrush, mountain brush, pinyon-juniper and up to spruce-fir communities from British Columbia to Colorado.

Comments: Unlike many other *Clematis* species, vase flower is not a vine. *Hirsutissima* (most hairy) defines the hairy leaves and stems. Some Native Americans used the root as a stimulant due to its bitter properties.

WOODS' ROSE
Rosa woodsii
Rose family (Rosaceae)

Description: Shrub to 7' tall; stems armed with spines or prickles. Compound leaves have 3–9 leaflets, ½–4" long, with toothed margins. Pinkish flowers are solitary or in small clusters; each flower is ½–2" wide. Fruit is red-orange to yellow and mealy.

Bloom Time: May to September.

Habitat/Range: Streamsides or riparian areas in mountain brush, pinyon-juniper, and spruce-fir communities across much of the West.

Comments: *Rosa* is the classical Latin name. Fruits are edible but seedy. Petals from the cultivated rose, *R. gallica*, provide the rose oil used in perfumes.

WRIGHT'S BIRDSBEAK
Cordylanthus wrightii
Figwort family (Scrophulariaceae)

Description: Annual, with stems 6–36" tall and many branched. Leaves, ⅜–1⅛" long, are often 3- to 5-lobed into narrow segments. Flowers, ½–1" long, have 3- to 5-lobed bracts beneath yellow to purple 2-lipped corolla. Corolla lips are unequal in length.

Bloom Time: July to October.

Habitat/Range: Blackbrush to pinyon-juniper communities, often in sandy soils, in the Southwest.

Comments: These plants bloom in late summer. *Cordylanthus* is from the Greek *kordyle* (club) and *anthos* (flower), referring to the shape of the flowers. The common name was inspired by the corolla's overlapping and unequal pair of lips, which resemble a bird's beak. *Wrightii* honors Charles Wright (1811–1885), a plant collector who participated on the Mexican Boundary Survey of 1849 and 1851–1852.

PINYON-JUNIPER LOUSEWORT
Pedicularis centranthera
Figwort family (Scrophulariaceae)

Description: Perennial, with stems 1½–2¼" tall. Leaves are divided to midrib, 2–6" long, linear to lance-shaped, and with "ruffled" toothed edges with white tips. Flowers grow in tight clusters; 5 lobes of calyx are of unequal lengths and slightly hairy. Corolla is purple or yellowish, ¾" long, and 2-lipped; upper lip is hooded and lower lip is 3-lobed.

Bloom Time: May to August.

Habitat/Range: Pinyon-juniper woodlands and mountain brush to ponderosa pine communities in the Southwest and north to Oregon.

Comments: *Pedicularis* (of lice) refers to the ancient use of the seeds to destroy lice. This lousewort is partially parasitic on other plants. *Centranthera* is from the Greek *centrum* (pointed) and *anther* (anthers).

PALMER'S PENSTEMON
Penstemon palmerii
Figwort family (Scrophulariaceae)

Description: Perennial with clustered stems, 2–5' tall. Thick leaves, ¾–4½" long, are elliptical and smooth. Flowers are pink to creamy white, inflated, with prominent wine-red nectar guidelines on inside of lower lip and prominent yellow "beard." Fruit is a capsule with numerous tiny seeds.

Bloom Time: May to September.

Habitat/Range: Mixed desert shrub, mountain brush, pinyon-juniper, and ponderosa pine communities. Originally found in southern Utah, but now more widespread.

Comments: *Penstemons* have bearded stamens, which give the genus another common name: beardtongue. The plant's inflated flowers indicate that bees and other insects, and also hummingbirds, pollinate this species. *Palmerii* is for Edward Palmer (1831–1911), an English immigrant who collected many native American bird and plant specimens in the West. Palmer's penstemon is now included in many commercial seed mixes—hence its expanded range.

GREEN AND/OR TINY FLOWERS

This section includes both green flowers and
the tiny, nonshowy, and/or unisexual flowers
of some of the tree species, as well as a
few grass species.

BOXELDER
Acer negundo
Maple family (Aceraceae)

Description: Medium-size, many-branched tree, 12–38' tall. Branchlets are smooth or velvet-hairy. Opposite leaves are compound with 3–7 coarsely toothed or lobed leaflets. Leaflets are ¾–4" long; the terminal leaflet is long-stemmed. Male and female flowers are borne separately in drooping tassels on separate trees. Fruit is a double-winged seed.

Bloom Time: March to May.

Habitat/Range: Riparian and marshy areas throughout the western United States and into Central America.

Comments: *Boxelder* is both from the "boxing" or tapping of the tree by settlers for its low-grade syrup and from the leaves' resemblance to those of the elderberry. *Acer* (maple) is the Latin name for these trees.

SPIDER MILKWEED
Asclepias asperula
Milkweed family (Asclepiadaceae)

Description: Perennial arising from a stout root. Stems may grow upright or trail along the ground. Plant is 10–20" tall and bears lance-shaped leaves, 5–10" long, that are pointed at the tip. Rounded flower clusters have greenish-white petals sometimes tinged with purple. Lobes are about ½" long. Greenish to purplish hoods are club- to sickle-shaped and abruptly curved from the anthers. Fruit is a slender pod 2–6" long.

Bloom Time: April to June.

Habitat/Range: Sandy sites or rocky openings in warm desert shrub and sagebrush flats to pinyon-juniper woodlands, mountain brush communities, and ponderosa pine forests from California to Texas.

Comments: *Asclepias* refers to Asklepios, a legendary Greek physician. *Asperula* (rough) refers to the texture of the leaves. The unique flowers are pollinated by a variety of insects.

PALLID MILKWEED
Asclepias cryptoceras
Milkweed family (Asclepiadaceae)

Description: Perennial plant, 4–12" long, with stems trailing along the ground. Opposite leaves are smooth and broadly oval, almost as long as broad. Flower clusters may or may not be short-stalked; individual flowers have greenish-white petals bent downward. Each lobe is about ½" long; 5 pouch-shaped hoods are pale rose. Seedpods are broadly spindle-shaped and up to 2¾" long.

Bloom Time: April to June.

Habitat/Range: Blackbrush, mixed desert shrub, and pinyon-juniper communities up to 6,240', from California to Colorado and north to Wyoming.

Comments: *Asclepias* refers to Asklepios, a human physician who was an authority on the medicinal properties of plants and who, according to Greek myth, could return the dead to life. Hades, the god of the dead, feared a loss of "employment" and coerced his brother Zeus into killing Asklepios with a thunderbolt. *Cryptoceras* (hidden horn) refers to the horn encased within the petals.

DWARF MILKWEED

Asclepias macrosperma
Milkweed family (Asclepiadaceae)

Description: Perennial, 2–10" long, with stems mostly reclining along the ground. Stems and leaves are densely covered with hairs. Short-stemmed, opposite leaves are egg-shaped, somewhat narrowly pointed at the end, and often folded longitudinally in half. Flower clusters located at the ends of stems have 5 greenish-white petals bent downward and 5 greenish-white pouch-shaped sacs. Seedpods are spindle-shaped, 1½–2½" long, and mostly smooth.

Bloom Time: April to June.

Habitat/Range: Mixed desert shrub up to pinyon-juniper communities in southern Utah and Arizona.

Comments: *Macrosperma* (large seed) refers to the size of the pods and seeds. Asklepios, a Greek physician, used a symbol of 1 or 2 serpents entwined about a staff, the caduceus, which is still the symbol for the medical profession today. This plant is also known as bigseed milkweed. This milkweed was first collected in 1893 in what would become Arches National Park.

OLD MAN SAGE

Artemisia filifolia
Sunflower family (Asteraceae)

Description: Silvery or grayish, highly branched shrub, 2–3' high or taller. Threadlike leaves are covered with small, dense hairs. Dense plumes of tiny, bell-shaped flowers form clusters that hang downward. Seeds are smooth and minute.

Bloom Time: July to October.

Habitat/Range: Sandy soils in shrublands and pinyon-juniper communities, 2,575–7,150', in the Southwest and north to South Dakota and into Mexico.

Comments: The wispy appearance of this shrub separates it from other species of sagebrush. Silvery leaves, wispy foliage, and the beardlike look of dense flower clusters give this plant its common name. *Artemisia* is from Artemisia, the wife of Mausolus, who was the ancient ruler of Caria (Southwest Asia Minor). She was named in honor of Artemis, the Greek virgin goddess of the hunt and of wild nature. *Filifolia* (threadlike leaves) describes the leaves.

LONGLEAF BRICKELLBUSH
Brickellia longifolia
Sunflower family (Asteraceae)

Description: Densely branched shrub, 3–6' tall. Alternate, stalkless leaves, ⅜–4¾" long, are narrow and gradually taper to a point. Flowers, 3–5 per cluster, are borne in many clusters along an elongated stalk at apex of the branch. Outer bracts below flower cluster are teardrop-shaped, while inner ones are long and slender. Small green flower heads bear only disk flowers; dried flowering stalks may overwinter.

Bloom Time: June to September.

Habitat/Range: Riparian areas, moist sites, and seeps in southern Utah. Also occurs from California to Arizona.

Comments: The genus is named for John Brickell (1749–1809), a physician and botanist from Savannah, Georgia. *Longifolia* (long leaves) describes the leaves.

WATER BIRCH
Betula occidentalis
Birch family (Betulaceae)

Description: Small tree or dense shrub to 20' tall; many with several main trunks. Bark is reddish or yellowish-brown, shiny, and marked with horizontal rows of thin holes. Leaves, broad and egg-shaped, are ½–3½" long with an abrupt point at the tip and doubly toothed margins. Unisexual flowers grow separately on the same plant; both are arranged in dense, hanging clusters. Fruit is a papery, conelike structure with tiny seeds.

Bloom Time: February to May.

Habitat/Range: Riparian areas from Alaska to Colorado.

Comments: *Occidentalis* (western) refers to this plant's geographical distribution in the western United States. Water birch grows in moist locations.

HALOGETON
Halogeton glomeratus
Goosefoot family (Chenopodiaceae)

Description: Annual weedy species that grows 1–20" tall. Alternate leaves are fleshy, ¼–¾" long, and with a slender spine at the tip. Small membranous flowers are borne in leaf axils and have egg-shaped bracts below. Stamens are grouped into 2 clusters with 2 or 3 stamens in each cluster. Fruit is a flattened seed.

Bloom Time: June to September.

Habitat/Range: Disturbed sites in salt desert shrub and pinyon-juniper communities throughout the western United States.

Comments: First introduced into northern Nevada in the early 1930s as an experimental forage crop (it failed, as it was too high in oxalates and therefore toxic to livestock), the plant quickly spread into the lower deserts of Nevada and Utah. *Halogeton* is from the Greek *halos* (salt) and *geiton* (neighbor); the plants grow well in saline soils.

140

RUSSIAN-THISTLE
Salsola tragus
Goosefoot family (Chenopodiaceae)

Description: Annual weed with red-purple stems to 3' or taller. Plants often branch near the base, and stems grow erect or curve upward. Narrow, linear leaves are ½–2¼" long and spine-tipped; smaller and more spinelike toward the top. Tiny flowers growing in short clusters are spiny. Fruit has papery disk surrounding the seed.

Bloom Time: May to July.

Habitat/Range: Disturbed sites throughout North America.

Comments: The classic Western weed, tumbleweed was first introduced into South Dakota around 1873 from Eurasia; the plant spread over the American West in a few decades. When the plant dies, the roots break off in the soil; as the detached plant "tumbles" in the wind, it breaks apart and spreads the seeds. Young shoots are salty, but edible. Tumbleweed is an indicator species of poor-quality rangeland.

UTAH JUNIPER

Juniperus osteosperma
Cypress family (Cupressaceae)

Description: Shrub or small tree with thin, fibrous bark that becomes shredded with age. Leaves are arranged oppositely or in whorls of threes, overlapping and scalelike, up to ¼" long, and slightly toothed along the margin. Juvenile plant's leaves are bluish-green and lance-shaped. Male and female cones are borne separately on the same plant. Seeds are enclosed in a hard shell within a bluish-gray waxy coating.

Bloom Time: March to June.

Habitat/Range: Riparian areas and shrublands, as well as pinyon-juniper woodlands and up into aspen communities from Montana to New Mexico.

Comments: Utah juniper is one of the two primary members of the pinyon-juniper plant community, which is a major and widespread habitat type in the Southwest. *Juniperus* is the Latin name for juniper, and *osteosperma* (hard seed) defines the seed shell. The female cone resembles a hard, bluish berry.

MORMON TEA

Ephedra viridis
Ephedra family (Ephedraceae)

Description: Shrub, 4–60" tall, with upright branches mainly bright green and smooth. Small, scalelike leaves located at the stem joints are arranged in pairs or sometimes in whorls. Male cones, 2 or more, are inversely egg-shaped and ¼" long. Female cones are inversely egg-shaped, up to ⅜" long, and with 4–8 pairs of rounded bracts. Brown seeds are borne in pairs.

Bloom Time: March to July.

Habitat/Range: Variety of shrubland communities up to mountain brush communities, 9,200'.

Comments: Steeping the branchlets makes a noncaffeinated tea that is used to treat colds and congestion. The commercial drug ephedrine (which is named for the genus) comes from *E. chinensis*, which grows in China. *Viridis* (green) refers to the plant's overall color.

GAMBEL'S OAK
Quercus gambelii
Beech family (Fagaceae)

Description: Deciduous shrub or small tree, to 30' tall, often growing in groves. Young leaves have dense star-shaped hairs on both sides, becoming, with age, greener and smooth above and hairy below. Leaf size is ¾–7"; individual leaves are elliptical or egg-shaped in outline and deeply lobed. Male and female flowers are borne separately in dense hanging clusters. Acorns are ½–¾" long.

Bloom Time: March to June.

Habitat/Range: Wide range of plant communities, from 3,500–8,560' in Wyoming.

Comments: Plants mainly propagate by cloning of underground stems. Native Americans collected the acorns, ground the nuts into flour, and soaked it in water to remove the bitter tannins. *Quercus* is Latin for oak. *Gambelii* honors William Gambel (1821–1849), an assistant curator at the Natural Academy of Sciences (now called the National Academy of Sciences) and an avid Western plant collector.

SHINNERY OAK
Quercus welshii
Beech family (Fagaceae)

Description: Deciduous shrub, 2–6' tall. Young leaves are densely hairy on both sides, becoming smoother with age. Leaves, ½–2½" long, are elliptical or inversely lance-shaped and often with 6–10 toothed lobes along the margin; lobes may be pointed or toothed again. Male and female flowers are borne separately in dense clusters that hang downward. Acorns are ½–¾" long.

Bloom Time: March to June.

Habitat/Range: Sandy soils in blackbrush and pinyon-juniper communities in the Southwest.

Comments: Complex root systems of the shinnery oak help stabilize sandy soils. *Welshii* honors Dr. Stanley L. Welsh (b. 1928), a botany professor at Brigham Young University and primary author of *A Utah Flora* and other wildflower books. The former common name was wavy-leaf oak.

WHITE-MARGINED SWERTIA
Swertia albomarginata
Gentian family (Gentianaceae)

Description: Perennial, 2–3' tall, with smooth, opposite, branching stems. Leaves, 1½–4" long, are arranged oppositely or in whorls of 4, have white margins, and are linear or inversely lance-shaped. Greenish-white flowers have 4 petals and sepals; petals have greenish dots and their lobes have a solitary gland fringed with short, soft white hairs.

Bloom Time: May to July.

Habitat/Range: Warm desert shrub up to mountain brush communities from California throughout the Southwest.

Comments: *Swertia* is for Emanuel Sweert, a sixteenth-century Dutch gardener and author. *Albomarginata* (white margin) refers to the conspicuous white edge of the leaf.

SHOWY GENTIAN
Swertia radiata
Gentian family (Gentianaceae)

Description: Perennial, often 4–6' tall. Basal leaves are spatula-shaped or elliptical, 8–20" long, and smooth or slightly hairy. Stem leaves are smaller and lance-shaped or inversely lance-shaped. Flowers are borne in whorled clusters; each flower, ⅜–¾" wide, has purplish dots on greenish petals and 2 glands on each petal's lobe.

Bloom Time: May to August.

Habitat/Range: Sagebrush, pinyon-juniper, mountain brush, and up to spruce-fir communities, from Washington to the Dakotas and south to Mexico.

Comments: Another common name is elkweed. The Navajo used to rub a cold tea made from the leaves on the bodies of hunters and horses to strengthen them for long expeditions. Dried leaves were mixed with tobacco and smoked.

COYOTE BUSH
Forestiera pubescens
Olive family (Oleaceae)

Description: Sprawling deciduous shrub, 6' tall or taller. Inversely lance-shaped or elliptical leaves, ½–2" long, sometimes have small serrations along the margin. Uni- or bisexual, inconspicuous flowers with yellowish stamens are borne on same plant, often before leaves mature. Blue-black fleshy fruit encases a hard seed.

Bloom Time: April to June.

Habitat/Range: Sandy sites along rivers and streams in the Canyonlands area. Grows from California to Texas and into Mexico.

Comments: Fruits are eaten by foxes and coyotes; hence the common name. Coyote bush grows in moist locations, especially along riverbanks, and is also called New Mexico privet or desert olive.

SINGLELEAF ASH
Fraxinus anomala
Olive family (Oleaceae)

Description: Deciduous shrub or small tree, 4–13' tall. Smooth leaves, ½–1½" long, are egg-shaped and slightly toothed or serrated along the margin. Tiny flowers lack petals, have orange anthers, and are borne in dense clusters in leaf axils. Each seed has one papery wing.

Bloom Time: April to June.

Habitat/Range: Blackbrush to ponderosa pine communities in the Southwest.

Comments: Settlers and Native Americans used the stout wood for tool handles and digging sticks. *Anomala* (anomaly) refers to this unique species of ash that has single, not compound, leaves.

HELLEBORINE
Epipactis gigantea
Orchid family (Orchidaceae)

Description: Perennial. Smooth, stout stems, 5–15", with tinge of purple at the base. Egg-shaped or elliptical leaves are broadest on lower portion of stem, narrower above, and 2–8" long. Showy flowers, ½–¾" wide, have greenish to rose-colored sepals with purple or dull red veins. Petals are brownish-purple; lower one is saclike and strongly marked with red or purple veins. Fruit is an elliptical capsule that hangs downward.

Bloom Time: May to August.

Habitat/Range: Riparian areas, seeps, and hanging gardens from British Columbia to Mexico and most of the western United States.

Comments: *Epipactis* (hellebore) is Greek for a different type of orchid. *Gigantea* (large) refers to the size of the plant and flowers. Orchids are unique in the hanging gardens and desert seeps.

ALCOVE BOG-ORCHID
Habenaria zothecina
Orchid family (Orchidaceae)

Description: Perennial, 7–24" tall. Leaves are elliptical or narrowly linear and long. Flowering stalk bears 5–20 green or yellowish-green flowers. Upper sepal is in close contact with petals and forms a hood over the style. Lateral sepals are curved and the petals triangularly lance-shaped. Lower petal (or "lip") is yellowish and linear.

Bloom Time: May to August.

Habitat/Range: Moist sites in seeps and hanging gardens in southeastern Utah.

Comments: *Habenaria* is from the Latin *habena* (reins or narrow strap), in reference to the narrow lip of the lower petal in some of the species. The overall green color of the plant makes this one difficult to find in greenery-rich hanging gardens and seeps.

147

TWO-NEEDLE PINYON
Pinus edulis
Pine family (Pinaceae)

Description: Small- to medium-size tree, mainly 15–45' tall. Yellowish-brown bark is thin and scaly, becoming furrowed and grayer with age. Evergreen needles, mostly 2 per cluster, are ⅜–2" long, rigid, and sharply pointed. Male cones are ⅛" long; resin-covered female cones are oval and up to 2" long. Seeds are brown to tan, thick-shelled, and wingless.

Bloom Time: June to August.

Habitat/Range: Pinyon-juniper and aspen communities from Wyoming to Mexico.

Comments: One of the two dominant trees of the pinyon-juniper plant community, this is the state tree of New Mexico. *Pinus* is the Latin name for pine, and *edulis* (edible) refers to the highly nutritive seeds. The sticky resin was used for waterproofing Native American baskets and pots, for gluing feathers to arrows, and for a host of other uses, some still in practice today.

PONDEROSA PINE
Pinus ponderosa
Pine family (Pinaceae)

Description: Tree that grows up to 125'; old-growth specimens may be massive. Bark on older trees becomes deeply furrowed and orangish in color. Long pine needles grow in clusters of 3 and may reach 4–10" long. Male and female cones are borne on same plant; larger female cones have a stout spine on the scales. Winged seeds are brownish-purple.

Bloom Time: April to June.

Habitat/Range: Mountain brush up to aspen communities, 3,800–8,300' throughout the West. Often forms expansive woodlands and may be mixed with other pine and coniferous species.

Comments: *Ponderosa* (large) describes the stature of these trees, which are harvested for their lumber. Numerous birds and small mammals consume the seeds or nest in the trees. The bark may give off an aroma of vanilla. One of several species of yellow pines, the ponderosa is also called western yellow pine or, in the case of old-growth trees, "pumpkins" after their orangish bark.

DOUGLAS FIR
Pseudotsuga menziesii
Pine family (Pinaceae)

Description: Stout tree with a massive trunk that may grow well over 100' tall. Bark changes from smooth to deeply furrowed and darker with age. Leaves are thin, 1–4" long, bluish-green in color, and arranged in whorls around the stem. Male and female cones are borne on same tree; female cones are mainly 3–4" long and have 3-lobed bracts that protrude beyond rounded scales.

Bloom Time: April to June.

Habitat/Range: Variety of soil conditions in canyons, mountain brush, and up to aspen communities across western North America, from British Columbia to Mexico.

Comments: *Pseudotsuga* (false *Tsuga*) refers to the tree's hemlock-like arrangement of needles. *Menziesii* honors Archibald Menzies (1754–1842), a surgeon and naturalist who sailed with the British explorer Captain George Vancouver from 1791 to 1795, and explored the west coast of North America. The common name honors David Douglas (1799–1834), a Scottish botanist who collected plants throughout the Pacific Northwest and Hawaii, where he died. Native Americans used the tree for building and firewood.

CHEATGRASS
Bromus tectorum
Grass family (Poaceae)

Description: Invasive and low-growing annual grass. Hollow stems are 6–24" tall, but may be taller depending on growing conditions. Smooth stems bear narrow leaf blades, 2–6" long, that are somewhat hairy; leaf sheath is also hairy. Compound flowering cluster is 2–6" long, slender, and droops to one side. Numerous individual spikelets are also hairy, ⅜ to ¾" long, and have 3–7 florets. Seeds have stiff awns.

Bloom Time: December to April.

Habitat/Range: Open and disturbed areas, 2,650–8,000', in a wide variety of habitats.

Comments: *Bromus* (oats) indicates the group of grasses this plant belongs to, and *tectorum* (of the roof) refers to the use of cheatgrass in roof thatching in olden days. A fire-adapted species, cheatgrass invades disturbed areas and is an indicator of poor rangeland health. The seeds become embedded in hiker's socks or animal fur and may fester or cause skin rashes.

NEEDLE-AND-THREAD GRASS
Stipa comata
Grass family (Poaceae)

Description: Perennial bunchgrass, up to 4' tall, that often grows in vast tracts. Basal leaves are narrow and roll inward along the margins and may be up to 12" long. Flowering stem is 4–8" long, narrow, and bears numerous tiny flowers. Sharp-pointed seeds have long, twisted awns.

Bloom Time: April and May.

Habitat/Range: Sandy soils from shrublands to mountain brush communities, 3,300–9,500', throughout the western United States.

Comments: The long seed awns and pointed seed reminded early botanists of a needle and thread combination; hence the common name. *Comata* (head of hair) refers to the tangled awns' resemblance to long hair strands. This is an important forage plant for wildlife.

INDIAN RICEGRASS
Stipa hymenoides
Grass family (Poaceae)

Description: Perennial bunchgrass that bears a widely spreading crown. Plants may be 2' tall. Slender leaf blades are 6–35" long and have either smooth or slightly hairy sheaths and smooth edges. Stems are hollow. Open, branching flower clusters are borne on thin stalks. Spikelets are up to 1" long and lower bracts are hairy. Seed is dark, round and about ⅛" long.

Bloom Time: May to August.

Habitat/Range: Sandy sites in shrublands up to ponderosa pine communities, 2,325–8,600', throughout the western United States.

Comments: *Stipa* (oakum) refers to the open feathery appearance of the flower clusters. *Hymenoides* (membranous) refers to the seed coverings. Native Americans harvested ricegrass seeds as a protein-rich food source.

LARGE-VALVE DOCK

Rumex venosus
Buckwheat family (Polygonaceae)

Description: Perennial that propagates from horizontally spreading roots. Stems are 4–20" tall; stem leaves are egg-shaped to elliptical, ¾–5½" long, and ⅜–2" wide. Numerous flowers have greenish floral segments, ¼" long; 3 segments become enlarged and red in fruit.

Bloom Time: April to July.

Habitat/Range: Dunes and other sandy sites, 4,270–6,950', throughout much of western North America.

Comments: *Venosus* (veined) refers to the prominent leaf veins. "Large-valve" refers to the large wings on the seeds. Boiling the roots produces red, yellow, or black dyes, depending on the material added to the roots. A poultice from mashed roots has been used to treat burns. Canaigre or wild rhubarb *(R. hymenosepalus)* has large, basal leaves and winged seeds.

DWARF MOUNTAIN MAHOGANY

Cercocarpus intricatus
Rose family (Rosaceae)

Description: Shrub, 1½–7' tall and intricately branched. Evergreen leaves, ⅛–¾" long, are narrow and linear with margins rolling inward; leaves are smooth or have short, appressed stiff hairs. Tiny flowers, about ⅛" long or smaller, lack petals and are solitary or in small clusters. Seeds have an elongated tail.

Bloom Time: April to June.

Habitat/Range: Rocky areas and slopes in pinyon-juniper, mountain brush, and ponderosa pine communities in the Southwest.

Comments: *Cercocarpus* is from the Greek *kerkos* (tail) and *carpos* (fruit), referring to the long feathery tails. *C. montanus*, the alder-leaf mountain mahogany, has deciduous leaves that resemble those of an alder, but has fruits similar to *C. intricatus*.

FREMONT'S COTTONWOOD
Populus fremontii
Willow family (Salicaceae)

Description: Tree that grows to 75' tall; broad, rounded crown in maturity. Bark is smooth and whitish on young tree; deeply furrowed and grayish or brown on older trunk. Leaves are triangular or heart-shaped, variously toothed along the margin, and have long petioles. Male and female flowers are borne separately on same tree in short clusters that appear before leaves in spring. Seeds are covered with fine white hairs.

Bloom Time: April to May.

Habitat/Range: Riparian areas and canyon bottoms throughout the Southwest.

Comments: The tree is named for the explorer, naturalist, and one-time presidential candidate John C. Frémont (1813–1890). Cottonwood seeds disperse after the spring runoff; seeds germinate

on the newly formed sandbars and their roots grow downward, following the lowering water table. The release of downy seeds in early summer resembles a snowfall.

COYOTE WILLOW
Salix exigua
Willow family (Salicaceae)

Description: Shrub growing in colonies, generally 6–9' tall with ashy gray stems. Branches are reddish and flexible; buds are covered by a single scale. Linear leaves, ¾–4½" long, are generally 10–20 times longer than wide and may have long silky hairs; leaf margins may be finely toothed. Clusters of separate male and female flowers may form as or after leaves develop. Fruit is a capsule.

Bloom Time: February to May.

Habitat/Range: Riparian areas and canyon bottoms up to 8,000' across much of North America.

Comments: *Salix* is the classic Latin name for willow. Native Americans used the flexible stems in basketry and in making split-willow figurines. *Exigua* (short) refers to the stature of this plant; however, some may attain 30' in height.

BROAD-LEAVED CATTAIL
Typha latifolia
Cattail family (Typhaceae)

Description: Aquatic perennial plant, 3–9' tall, with strapped-shaped leaves as long as the flowering stalk. Long, rounded flowering stalk bears fuzzy-brown, dense cluster of flowers near the top. Male flowers are located above female flowers and separated by a small gap.

Bloom Time: March to June.

Habitat/Range: Marshy areas, isolated rock pools, and slow-moving water areas throughout much of North America.

Comments: *Typha* is the Greek name for these plants. *Latifolia* (broad-leaved) refers to the width of the leaves. Native Americans harvested the roots, seeds, and pollen for food and the leaves for weaving sleeping mats.

NETLEAF HACKBERRY
Celtis reticulata
Elm family (Ulmaceae)

Description: Small tree, 15–20' tall, with a spreading canopy. Bark is veined with corky ridges at maturity. Leaves are egg- or lance-shaped, rounded at the base, rough on the surface, toothed along the margin, and typically infested with insect galls. Flowers are minute and inconspicuous; spherical fruits are reddish to orange or dark red, fleshy, and sweet.

Bloom Time: March to May.

Habitat/Range: Riparian areas, hanging gardens, and other moist sites from the Northwest to Mexico.

Comments: Fruits are edible and mostly eaten by mammals. *Reticulata* (netlike) refers to the intricate venation of the leaves; the derivation of *celtis* is obscure.

JUNIPER MISTLETOE
Phoradendron juniperinum
Mistletoe family (Viscaceae)

Description: Partially parasitic plant that grows on junipers. Dense cluster of stout stems with swollen joints arises from branches of juniper; stems are 6–15" long. Greenish-yellow stems have tiny scalelike leaves. Male and female flowers are borne on separate plants and are greenish to greenish-yellow. Fruit is 1-seeded, fleshy, and pinkish.

Bloom Time: July to August.

Habitat/Range: Mainly parasitic on Utah juniper. Range is from Oregon to Texas and into Mexico.

Comments: *Phoradendron* is from *phor* (thief) and *dendron* (tree) and refers to the plant's tendency to steal nutrients from its host. *Juniperinum* (on junipers) refers to this plant's preference for parasitizing junipers. Birds consume the fleshy fruits and pass the seeds intact through their digestive tracts as one means of seed dispersal.

BLUE FLOWERS

Bluish flowers often grade into other hues,
so you should also check the pink and purple
flower section.

CHICORY

Cichorum intybus
Sunflower family (Asteraceae)

Description: A perennial plant that grows 2–5' tall on stems that are smooth or hairy. Stems exude thin, milky sap when broken. Basal leaves are alternate, 3–10" long, and toothed along margins. Leaves become smaller up the stem. Beautifully colored large flower heads bear only ray flowers that are blue, lavender, or sometimes white. Rays are lobed at tips. Fruit is a small seed.

Bloom Time: June to October.

Habitat/Range: Disturbed sites along roadsides and a wide variety of habitats, 2,850–6,650', across much of North America. Native to Eurasia.

Comments: *Cichorium* is derived from the Arabic name of the plant. *Intybus* comes from the Latin *tybi* (January), which refers to the time period when these plants were eaten. The ground roots are used as a coffee substitute.

UTAH DAISY

Erigeron utahensis
Sunflower family (Asteraceae)

Description: Perennial, up to 2' high, with stems appearing grayish or silvery due to short, stiff hairs. Withered leaves may be present at base. Lower leaves, ⅜–4" long, are narrow and linear to wider at tips; upper leaves are smaller. Flower heads, ½" wide, are solitary or in clusters with 10–40 bluish or white rays surrounding dense cluster of yellowish disk flowers. Seeds have a double row of bristles.

Bloom Time: April to July.

Habitat/Range: Salt and warm desert shrub, pinyon-juniper, and mountain brush communities in the Southwest.

Comments: The type specimen of this species was collected near Kanab, Utah; thus the name *utahensis* (of Utah).

SILVERY LUPINE
Lupinus argenteus
Pea family (Fabaceae)

Description: Perennial, 7–34" tall. Stems and leaf petioles have soft or stiff hairs. Compound leaves, ½–3" long, have 6–9 spatula- or inversely lance-shaped leaflets that have short, stiff hairs on both sides or are smooth above. Large flowering stalks bear 15–92 bluish-purple flowers, ⅜–¾" long, the upper petal having a central yellow or white spot. Pods may be hairy or smooth and contain 3–6 seeds.

Bloom Time: April to June.

Habitat/Range: Various desert shrub, pinyon-juniper, ponderosa pine, and aspen communities from Washington to Kansas.

Comments: *Lupinus* is from the Latin *lupus* (wolf), in reference to the plants "wolfing" or taking nourishment from the soil. When mature, the seedpods split open and eject the seeds to aid with dispersal.

DWARF LUPINE
Lupinus pusillus
Pea family (Fabaceae)

Description: Annual, up to 9" tall, with long, spreading hairs on stems and leaf petioles. Leaflets, 3–9, are inversely lance-shaped, ½–1½" long, flat or folded, and smooth above with long, soft hairs below. Flower stalk bears 4–38 bluish or bicolored flowers, ¼–½" long; upper petal has a yellow spot. Seedpods are fairly oval, with constrictions between seeds.

Bloom Time: April to June.

Habitat/Range: Various desert shrub and pinyon-juniper communities, 2,500–6,150', from Washington to California and throughout the Southwest.

Comments: *Pusillus* (dwarf) refers to the small stature of these plants. The sandy soils where they often grow make a photogenic contrast between the blue flowers and the reddish sand. Dwarf lupine is pollinated by bees.

SILVERY SOPHORA
Sophora stenophylla
Pea family (Fabaceae)

Description: Perennial, 4–16" tall. Lacy leaves alternate, linear to oblong, and are covered with dense, soft silvery hairs. Terminal flowering stalks have 12–39 blue or bluish-purple, pea-shaped flowers. Pods have 1–5 seeds and short, stiff hairs lying closely against surface.

Bloom Time: April and May.

Habitat/Range: Sandy sites in blackbrush, pinyon-juniper, and ponderosa pine communities in southern Utah, New Mexico, and Arizona.

Comments: The lacy foliage and flower color make this is a very distinct plant. Herbage and seeds are toxic to livestock if eaten in large quantities. Silvery sophora colonizes areas by underground horizontal roots.

WILD IRIS
Iris missouriensis
Iris family (Iridaceae)

Description: Perennial up to 3' tall, arising from thick root. Long, straplike leaves are smooth, and there may be several or many leaves per plant. Flowering stalk is about as long as leaves and bears 1–3 bluish-purple flowers. Three outside sepals droop and have distinct veins. Upright petals are broad. Three additional petal-like structures are pistils. Fruit is a capsule.

Bloom Time: May to July.

Habitat/Range: Wet meadows, fields, and along streams in sagebrush, mountain brush, and higher communities from British Columbia to the Southwest.

Comments: *Iris* honors the Greek goddess Iris, whose message-bearing appearance was often preceded by a rainbow. *Missouriensis* (of the Missouri) refers to when Meriwether Lewis first collected this plant along the Missouri River. Native Americans pulverized the roots of wild iris to treat toothaches. This plant often grows in abundance, creating spectacular displays.

BLUE FLAX
Linum perenne
Flax family (Linaceae)

Description: Perennial from stout taproot, arising on stems to 2½' tall. Basal leaves are linear, up to 1¼" long, and in a whorled pattern; upper leaves are smaller. Blue or bluish-white flowers have yellowish centers and are 1" wide. Five papery petals are short-lived, often falling off within a day. Fruit is a small, squat globe containing small dark seeds.

Bloom Time: April to July,

Habitat/Range: Sagebrush flats, pinyon-juniper woodlands, and up to spruce-fir communities from Alaska to Mexico.

Comments: *L. perenne* was originally called *L. lewisii* in honor of the Western explorer Meriwether Lewis. Cultivated flax, from which linen thread and linseed oil are manufactured, is a close relative. Blue flax does extremely well in cultivated gardens. *Perenne* (perennial) indicates the plant's longevity.

NAKED BROOMRAPE
Orobanche uniflora
Broomrape family (Orobanchaceae)

Description: Fleshy, parasitic plant, 1–4" tall. Basal leaves are lance-shaped and up to ½" long. Long, yellowish flowering stalk arises from leaves and is covered with sticky hairs. Single flower is borne at end of stalk; tubular flower is bluish or purple, has 2 prominent yellow ridges on lower lip, and is about 2" long. Protruding stamens may be smooth or woolly. Fruit is a capsule.

Bloom Time: April to July.

Habitat/Range: Moist meadows, grasslands, sagebrush, pinyon-juniper, and up to higher plant communities across much of North America.

Comments: *Orobanche* is from *orobos* (a type of vetch or climbing plant); *ancho* (to strangle) refers to its parasitic nature. *Uniflora* (one flower) refers to the solitary flower. Parasitic to sagebrush and other plants, this small flower may be easily overlooked.

ANDERSON'S LARKSPUR
Delphinium andersonii
Buttercup family (Ranunculaceae)

Description: Perennial, 4–24" tall. Stems are mostly smooth and arise from basal cluster of leaves; few leaves may be present along lower portion of stem. Leaf blades, ⅜–2⅜" wide, are usually divided 3 times. Flowers, 1–15, are borne along elongated axis; 5 petal-like sepals bluish, 2 lower petals spreading and broad, and the upper one forming a prominent spur.

Bloom Time: April to July.

Habitat/Range: Blackbrush, salt desert shrub, and pinyon-juniper communities in the Southwest and north to Oregon.

Comments: *Delphinium* (like a dolphin) refers to the shape of the flower buds. The plant contains the alkaloid delphinine, which is very toxic to livestock. After flowering, the toxicity of the alkaloid diminishes. Another common name is pale larkspur.

DUSTY PENSTEMON

Penstemon comarrhenus
Figwort family (Scrophulariaceae)

Description: Tall perennial with smooth stems that grows 1–4' high. Basal leaves are inversely lance-shaped, opposite, and ¾–5" long. Few stem leaves are linear and smaller. Flowers are pale blue, ¾–1½" long, 2-lipped, and tubular. Hairy anther sacs are visible inside flower's throat. Throat may be pale blue, lavender, or whitish. Fruit is a small capsule.

Bloom Time: May to July.

Habitat/Range: Pinyon-juniper, mountain brush, ponderosa pine, and Douglas fir–aspen communities in the Southwest, 5,300–8,580'.

Comments: *Penstemon* is from the Greek *pen* (almost) and *stemon* (thread), referring to the stamens. Only 4 of the 5 stamens produce pollen, so the fifth is "almost a stamen." Bees are the primary pollinators of these flowers.

BLUESTEM PENSTEMON
Penstemon cyanocaulis
Figwort family (Scrophulariaceae)

Description: Perennial that arises on stems 10–22" tall. Smooth stems bear inversely lance-shaped leaves that are 1–6" long and narrow. Dense cluster of flowers arises along elongated stalk. Two-lipped, blue to lavender-blue flowers are ½–1" long and tubular in shape. Fruit is a woody capsule.

Bloom Time: April to July.

Habitat/Range: Blackbrush, pinyon-juniper, and mountain brush communities up to 7,200' in southeastern Utah and southwestern Colorado.

Comments: *Cyanocaulis* is from cyan (blue) and *caulis* (stem), referring to the color of the stem. This plant often grows in profusion. Bees and other flying insects pollinate the flowers.

ORANGE AND RED FLOWERS

This section contains orange and red flowers found in the Canyonlands region.

BUTTERFLY-WEED
Asclepias tuberosa
Milkweed family (Asclepiadaceae)

Description: Bushy herbaceous perennial to 3' tall; stout stems covered with small, coarse hairs. Sap is clear. Narrow, short-stemmed leaves are lance- to dagger-shaped and approximately 4" long. Lower leaves alternate; upper leaves may be opposite. Flower clusters have about 25 small-stalked, orange to yellowish-red flowers, each with 5 reflexed petals and 5 erect hoods. Spindle-shaped pods, up to 6" long, have small, soft hairs.

Bloom Time: May to July.

Habitat/Range: Sagebrush, pinyon-juniper, mountain brush, and ponderosa pine communities from Minnesota south to Mexico and the Southwest.

Comments: *Tuberosa* (swollen) refers to the thickened roots, which are used to treat lung ailments; another common name for this plant is pleurisy-root. Butterfly-weed is found in modern herbal teas. Unlike many milkweed species, butterfly-weed does not have a milky sap. When in bloom, the uniquely colored flowers attract numerous bees, butterflies, and other insects.

CLARETCUP
Echinocereus triglochidiatus
Cactus family (Cactaceae)

Description: Few to several hundred stems in compact hemisphere clumps or mounds. Stems are mainly cylindrical, up to 1' long and 1–2½" thick, with 9 or 10 ribs. Central spines are straight or slightly curved, 1–1½" long; radial spines are smaller. Flowers are scarlet and fruits red at maturity.

Bloom Time: March to June.

Habitat/Range: Various grasslands and shrublands, pinyon-juniper, and up to mountain brush communities from California to Texas and south into Mexico.

Comments: *Echinocereus* is from the Greek *echinos* (hedgehog), referring to this plant's resemblance to the animal. *Triglochidiatus* refers to the straight spines arranged in clusters of 3. Fruits are edible.

COMMON GLOBEMALLOW

Sphaeralcea coccinea
Mallow family (Malvaceae)

Description: Perennial, with stems solitary or many from woody base, 2–18" tall. Leaf blades are longer than wide; 3–5 deep lobes may be again lobed or toothed. Orange to scarlet flowers, ½" wide with numerous stamens, are borne along elongated stalk. Rounded capsule contains numerous tiny black seeds.

Bloom Time: April to July.

Habitat/Range: Grasslands, shrublands, and up to ponderosa pine communities from Canada to the Southwest.

Comments: *Sphaeralcea*, from *sphaira* (globe) and *alcea* (the name of a related genus), refers to the spherical fruits. *Coccinea* (scarlet) refers to the floral color. Sometimes bees of the genus *Diadaysia* can be found in the morning curled up in the flowers. Slender gooseberry (*S. leptophylla*) has narrow leaves.

GOOSEBERRY-LEAVED GLOBEMALLOW

Sphaeralcea grossularifolia
Mallow family (Malvaceae)

Description: Perennial, up to 3' tall, often with numerous stems arising from woody base. Stem and leaves may have white hairs. Leaf blades are heart- to wedge-shaped with wider base, 3 to 5 deep lobes, and irregularly toothed margins. Orangish-red flowers are arranged in tight clusters, and each flower is ½–1" wide. Fruit is a round capsule.

Bloom Time: May to July.

Habitat/Range: Salt desert shrub, pinyon-juniper, and ponderosa pine communities from Washington to California and across the Southwest.

Comments: *Grossularifolia* refers to the leaves' resemblance to those of gooseberries. *S. parviflora*, small-leaf globemallow, also grows in profusion and at times blankets large patches of ground.

CARMINE GILIA
Gilia subnuda
Phlox family (Polemoniaceae)

Description: Biennial or perennial, 6–20" tall, with basal rosette of leaves with sticky hairs. Leaves are spatula- to egg-shaped, variously lobed, and ¾–3¾" long. Reddish or carmine flowers cluster at ends of thin stems; corolla tube, ⅜–¾" long, flares to 5 lobes at opening.

Bloom Time: May to July.

Habitat/Range: Warm desert shrub, pinyon-juniper, and ponderosa pine communities across the Southwest.

Comments: The sticky hairs tend to catch blowing sand; thus the leaves and stems may have a sandy coating. Also called sand gilia, the flowers are pollinated by hummingbirds and butterflies.

SCARLET GILIA
Ipomopsis aggregata
Phlox family (Polemoniaceae)

Description: Biennial or perennial, with stems arising from basal rosette of leaves that are deeply lobed with narrow segments. Stems, 40" or taller, have sticky or white hairs. Stem leaves are similar to basal ones but smaller. Reddish flowers borne in loose clusters are ¾–1½" long with a long, narrow tube and pointed, flaring lobes.

Bloom Time: April to September.

Habitat/Range: Riparian, sagebrush, pinyon-juniper, and ponderosa pine communities up to spruce-fir habitats from British Columbia to the Southwest.

Comments: Formerly called *Gilia aggregata*, *Gilia* was for Filippo Luigi Gilii (1756–1821), a scientist and astronomer; *aggregata* (clustered) refers to the close arrangement of the flowers. Plants may have a skunklike odor. *Ipomopsis* (similar to *Ipomea*) refers to the flowers' resemblance to those of another genus.

COMMON PAINTBRUSH
Castilleja chromosa
Figwort family (Scrophulariaceae)

Description: Perennial, 4–20" tall; stems clustered and with fine hairs. Lower leaves are linear or lance-shaped; upper leaves have 1–3 lobes. All leaves have fine, stiff hairs. Flower-like bracts are reddish and tubular; cleft calyx lobes have rounded segments. Corolla is green and 2-lipped, the upper lip beaklike and the lower lip shorter and 3-toothed.

Bloom Time: March to June.

Habitat/Range: Desert shrub and pinyon-juniper communities, 2,650–8,675', in the Southwest and north to Oregon.

Comments: *Castilleja* is for Domingo Castillejo, an eighteenth-century Spanish botanist. *Chromosa* (red) describes the color of the flower's bracts. Common paintbrush is partially parasitic on the roots of other plants.

ANNUAL PAINTBRUSH
Castilleja exilis
Figwort family (Scrophulariaceae)

Description: Annual, with erect stems 4–36" tall that have sticky, long straight hairs. Leaves are linear and narrow to a point. Flowers are borne along elongated stalk; bracts are scarlet for half their length. Fruit is a capsule.

Bloom Time: June to October.

Habitat/Range: Moist locations such as seeps, hanging gardens, wetlands, springs, along river courses or streamsides from the Northwest to the Southwest.

Comments: This is the only annual species of *Castilleja* in the region. The flowers resemble a paintbrush dipped in red paint, hence the common name. Paintbrushes are pollinated by hummingbirds.

WYOMING PAINTBRUSH
Castilleja linariifolia
Figwort family (Scrophulariaceae)

Description: Perennial, 8–32". Grasslike or lance-shaped leaves are ⅜–4" long; some have several pairs of narrow lobes. Conspicuous flowers have scarlet bracts with 1–2 pairs of deeply divided lobes that sit below 2-lipped corolla. Corolla is greenish and rises above bracts.

Bloom Time: May to September.

Habitat/Range: Riparian or moist habitats in sagebrush, pinyon-juniper, mountain brush, and ponderosa pine communities from Oregon to New Mexico.

Comments: This semiparasitic paintbrush is the state flower of Wyoming. *Linariifolia* (with leaves like *Linaria*) refers to the narrow leaves, which resemble those of *Linaria*, another member of the figwort family.

SCARLET MONKEYFLOWER
Mimulus eastwoodiae
Figwort family (Scrophulariaceae)

Description: Perennial, up to 15" tall with stout rounded stems. Leaves are arranged oppositely; upper leaves are dark green, elliptical to broadly lance-shaped, toothed along margins, deeply veined, and pointed at tips. Calyx has 5 angular, pointed lobes; dried calyx may overwinter. Reddish tubular corolla, 1" long, flares open at mouth. Flowers are 2-lipped, but the lips are unequal.

Bloom Time: May to August.

Habitat/Range: Seeps or hanging gardens in the Southwest.

Comments: *Mimulus* is from the Latin *mimus* (mimic), referring to the flowers' mimicking of a monkey's face or possibly to the monkey-like resemblance of the plant hanging from alcove ceilings. *Eastwoodiae* is for Alice Eastwood (1859–1953), a curator of botany at the California Academy of Sciences.

EATON'S PENSTEMON
Penstemon eatonii
Figwort family (Scrophulariaceae)

Description: Robust perennial, to 40" tall or more, with few to several stems from short woody base. Basal leaves are clustered, smooth, dark green, wavy along margins, and 1–7" long. Leaf blades are broad, narrowing at base. Red tubular flowers, 1–1½" long, hang downward and may flare open slightly at tips.

Bloom Time: April to July.

Habitat/Range: Variety of habitat types, 2,750–7,150', mainly in the Southwest.

Comments: *Penstemon* is from the Greek *pen* (almost) and *stemon* (thread), referring to the stamens. *Eatonii* is for David Cady Eaton (1834–1885), an American botanist. Hummingbirds and butterflies pollinate the tubular flowers.

UTAH PENSTEMON
Penstemon utahensis
Figwort family (Scrophulariaceae)

Description: Perennial, with smooth stems 6–24" tall. Leaves are thick and leathery, rounded to obtuse at tips. Basal leaves, ¾–4" long, are spatulate to broadly inversely lance-shaped. Stem leaves are smaller and more lance-shaped. Flowers are reddish; corolla tube is ½–¾" long with lobes spread flat at opening.

Bloom Time: April to June.

Habitat/Range: Mixed desert shrub, sagebrush, and pinyon-juniper communities from Utah to California.

Comments: *Utahensis* (of Utah) refers to the origin of the type specimen, which was found near Monticello, Utah. The flowers are pollinated by hummingbirds and butterflies.

GLOSSARY

Alternate—placed singly along a stem or axis, one after another, usually each successive item on a different side from the previous; often used in reference to the arrangement of leaves on a stem (*see* Opposite).

Annual—a plant completing its life cycle, from seed germination to production of new seeds, within a year, and then dying.

Axil—the area created on the upper side of the angle between leaf and stem.

Basal—at the base or bottom of; generally used in reference to leaves arranged at the base of the plant.

Biennial—a plant completing its life cycle in two years and normally not producing flowers during the first year.

Bract—reduced or modified leaf, often associated with flowers.

Bristle—a stiff hair, usually erect or curving away from its attachment point.

Bulb—underground plant part derived from a short, usually rounded, shoot that is covered with scales or leaves.

Calyx—the outer set of flower parts, composed of the sepals, which may be separate or joined together; usually green.

Capsule—a dry fruit that releases seeds through splits or holes.

Cluster—any grouping or close arrangement of individual flowers that is not dense and continuous.

Compound Leaf—a leaf that is divided into two to many leaflets, each of which may look like a complete leaf, but which lacks buds. Compound leaves may have leaflets arranged along an axis like the rays of a feather or radiating from a common point like the fingers on a hand (*see* illustration p. 13).

Corolla—the set of flower parts interior to the calyx and surrounding the stamens, composed of the petals, which may be free or united; often brightly colored.

Deciduous—broad-leaved trees or shrubs that drop their leaves at the end of each growing season, as contrasted with plants that retain their leaves throughout the year (*see* Evergreen).

Disk Flower—small, tubular flowers in the central portion of the flower head of many plants in the sunflower family (Asteraceae) (*see* illustration p. 17).

Elliptical (leaf shape)—*see* illustration p. 14

Entire (leaf margin)—*see* illustration p. 14

Evergreen—plants that bear green leaves throughout the year, as contrasted with plants that lose their leaves at the end of the growing season (*see* Deciduous).

Family—a group of plants having biologically similar features, such as flower anatomy, fruit type, etc.

Flower Head—as used in this guide, a dense and continuous group of flowers, without obvious branches or space between them; used especially in reference to the sunflower family (Asteraceae).

Genus—a group of closely related species, such as the genus *Penstemon* encompassing the penstemons (*see* Specific Epithet).

Herbaceous—a term that refers to any nonwoody plant; often reserved for wildflowers.

Hood—curving or folded, petal-like structures interior to the petals and exterior to the stamens in milkweed (Asclepiadaceae) flowers; since most milkweeds have reflexed petals, the hoods are typically the most prominent feature of the flowers.

Inflorescence—generally a cluster of flowers, although there are many terms to specifically describe the arrangement of flowers on the plant.

Involucre—a distinct series of bracts or leaves that subtend a flower or cluster of flowers. Often used in the description of the sunflower family (Asteraceae) flower heads.

Keel—a sharp lengthwise fold or ridge, referring particularly to the two fused petals forming the lower lip in many flowers of the pea family (Fabaceae).

Lance (leaf shape)—*see* illustration p. 14

Leaflet—a distinct, leaflike segment of a compound leaf.

Linear (leaf shape)—*see* illustration p. 14

Lobe—a segment of an incompletely divided plant part, typically rounded; often used in reference to the leaves.

Midrib—the central or main vein of a leaf.

Node—the region of the stem where one or more leaves are attached. Buds are commonly borne at the node, in the axils of the leaves.

Nutlet—a descriptive term for small nutlike fruits. Used to describe the separate lobes of a mature ovary in the borage and mint families.

Oblong (leaf shape)—*see* illustration p. 14

Opposite—paired directly across from one another along a stem or axis (*see* Alternate).

Ovary—the portion of the flower where the seeds develop, usually a swollen area below the style (if present) and stigma.

Pappus—in the sunflower family (Asteraceae) the modified limb of the calyx is the pappus and consists of a crown of bristles, hairs, or scales at the top of the seed.

Parallel—side by side, approximately the same distance apart for the entire length; often used in reference to veins or edges of leaves.

Perennial—a plant that normally lives for three or more years.

Petal—component part of the corolla; often the most brightly colored and visible part of the flower.

Petiole—the stalk of a leaf. The length of the petiole may be used in leaf descriptions.

Pinnate—a compound leaf, like many of the pea family (Fabaceae) members, where smaller leaflets are arranged along either side of a common axis.

Pistil—the seed-producing, or female, part of a flower, consisting of the ovary, style (if present), and stigma; a flower may have one to several separate pistils.

Pollen—tiny, often powdery male reproductive cells formed in the stamens and typically necessary for seed production.

Ray Flower—flower in the sunflower family (Asteraceae) with a single, strap-shaped corolla, resembling one flower petal; several to many ray flowers may surround the disk flowers in a flower head, or in some species such as dandelions, the flower heads may be composed entirely of ray flowers (*see* illustration p. 17).

Rosette—a dense cluster of basal leaves from a common underground part, often in a flattened, circular arrangement.

Scale—any thin, membranous body that resembles to some extent the scales of fish or reptiles.

Sepal—component part of the calyx; typically green but sometimes enlarged and brightly colored.

Shrub—a perennial woody plant of relatively low height, and typically with several stems arising from or near the ground.

Simple Leaf—a leaf that has a single leafllike blade, although this may be lobed or divided.

Spatulate (leaf shape)—*see* illustration p. 14

Specific Epithet—the second portion of a scientific name, identifying a particular species; for instance in fourwing saltbush, *Atriplex canescens*, the specific epithet is *canescens*.

Spike—an elongated, unbranched cluster of stalkless or nearly stalkless flowers.

Stalk—as used here, the stem supporting the leaf, flower, or flower cluster.

Stalkless—lacking a stalk; a stalkless leaf is attached directly to the stem at the leaf base.

Stamen—the male unit of a flower, which produces the pollen; typically consisting of a long filament with a pollen-producing tip.

Standard—the usually erect, spreading upper petal in many flowers of the pea family (Fabaceae).

Stigma—portion of the pistil receptive to pollination; usually at the top of the style, and often appearing fuzzy or sticky.

Style—the portion of the pistil between the ovary and the stigma; typically a slender stalk.

Subtend—situated below or beneath, often encasing or enclosing something.

Toothed—bearing teeth, or sharply angled projections, along the edge.

Variety—a group of plants within a species that has a distinct range, habitat, structure.

Whorl—three or more parts attached at the same point along a stem or axis and often surrounding the stem.

Wings—the two side petals flanking the keel in many flowers of the pea family (Fabaceae).

SELECTED REFERENCES

Blackwell, Laird R. 2006. *Great Basin Wildflowers: A Guide to Common Wildflowers of the High Deserts of Nevada, Utah, and Oregon.* Guilford, CT: Globe Pequot Press.

Coffey, Timothy. 1993. *The History and Folklore of North American Wildflowers.* New York: Facts-on-File.

Comstock, Jonathan P., and James R. Ehleringer. 1992. "Plant Adaptation in the Great Basin and Colorado Plateau." *Great Basin Naturalist* 52(3): 195–215.

Dunmire, William W., and Gail D. Tierney. 1995. *Wild Plants of the Pueblo Province: Exploring Ancient and Enduring Uses.* Santa Fe: Museum of New Mexico Press.

Elmore, Francis H. 1976. *Shrubs and Trees of the Southwest Uplands.* Globe, AZ: Southwest Parks and Monuments Association.

Harrington, H. D., and L. W. Durrell. 1979. *How to Identify Plants.* 1957. Reprint, Athens: University of Ohio Press, Swallow Press.

Heil, Kenneth D., J. Mark Porter, Rich Fleming, and William H. Romme. 1993. *Vascular Flora and Vegetation of Capitol Reef National Park, Utah.* United States Department of the Interior National Park Service Technical Report NPS/NAUCARE/NRTR 93/01.

Hitchcock, C. Leo, and Arthur Cronquist. 1973. *Flora of the Pacific Northwest.* Seattle: University of Washington Press.

Howe, Henry F., and Lynn C. Westley. 1988. *Ecological Relationships of Plants and Animals.* New York: Oxford University Press.

Kricher, John C., and Gordon Morrison. 1993. *A Field Guide to the Ecology of Western Forests.* Boston: Houghton Mifflin.

Leake, Dorothy Van Dyke, John B. Leake, and Marcelotte Leake Roeder. 1993. *Desert and Mountain Plants of the Southwest.* Norman: University of Oklahoma Press.

Louw, Gideon, and Mary Seely. 1982. *Ecology of Desert Organisms.* London: William Clowes.

MacMahon, James. 1985. *Deserts.* Audubon Society Nature Guide. New York: Alfred A. Knopf.

Proctor, Michael, and Peter Yeo. 1972. *The Pollination of Flowers.* New York: Taplinger Publishing.

Rahm, David A. 1974. *Reading the Rocks: A Guide to the Geologic Secrets of Canyons, Mesas and Buttes of the American Southwest.* San Francisco: Sierra Club Books.

Santillo, Humbart. 1985. *Natural Healing with Herbs.* Prescott Valley, AZ: Hohm Press.

Sounders, Charles F. 1933. *Western Wild Flowers and Their Stories.* Garden City, NY: Doubleday, Doran.

Tweit, Susan J. 1992. *The Great Southwest Nature Factbook.* Seattle: Alaska Northwest Books.

Welsh, Stanley L., N. Duane Atwood, Sherel Goodrich, and Larry C. Higgins. 1993. *A Utah Flora.* Provo, UT: Brigham Young University.

Williams, David B. A. 2000. *A Naturalist's Guide to Canyon Country.* Guilford, CT: Falcon-Guides.

Wormwood, Valerie A. 1991. *The Complete Book of Essential Oils and Aromatherapy.* San Rafael, CA: New World Library.

Zwinger, Ann H. 1989. *The Mysterious Lands: A Naturalist Explores the Four Great Deserts of the Southwest.* Tucson: University of Arizona Press.

INDEX

ABOUT THE AUTHOR

Damian Fagan is a naturalist residing in central Oregon with his wife, Raven, and daughter, Luna Sierra. He completed a B.S. in Botany from the University of Washington in 1982, then moved to Moab, Utah, to work for the National Park Service as a seasonal park ranger. In 1991 he founded BUTEO Wildlife Consultants, specializing in population inventories and project clearances on the avian fauna of the Colorado Plateau for private organizations and government agencies. When not out birding, he writes natural history articles and photographs the inhabitants of the Canyonlands region and Pacific Northwest.

CANYONLANDS NATURAL HISTORY ASSOCIATION

Canyonlands Natural History Association (CNHA) was established in 1967 as a not-for-profit organization to assist the scientific, educational, and visitor service efforts of the National Park Service (NPS), the Bureau of Land Management (BLM), and US Forest Service (USFS).

CNHA's goals include enhancing each visitor's understanding and appreciation of public lands by providing a thorough selection of quality educational materials for sale in its bookstore outlets. A portion of CNHA's proceeds, including profit from this publication, are returned directly to our public land partners to fund their educational, research, and scientific programs. Bookstore sales support the agencies' programs in various ways, including free publications, outdoor education programs for local school districts, equipment and supplies for ranger/naturalists, exhibits, and funds for research. Since our inception in 1967, CNHA has donated over 8 million dollars to our public land partners.

The Discovery Pool

CNHA established The Discovery Pool in 2006 to provide our federal partners with financial support for eligible scientific studies conducted within their administrative boundaries.

The goals for use of the Discovery Pool grants are:

- Encourage the scientific research that makes up the backbone of interpretive and educational programs, including resource management or protection surveys and monitoring.
- Provide matching funds that may assist federal partners in obtaining larger grants.
- Promote an understanding of the intricate cultural and natural resource complexities found on federally administered lands.

CNHA Membership

People protect that which they understand. With visitor use demands escalating and agency funding declining, CNHA's role in assisting in the agencies' educational efforts will continue to expand. Those wishing to support CNHA and our mission are invited to join the association's membership program. (Membership dues and other contributions are tax deductible to the extent provided by law.)

For more information about CNHA, the Discovery Pool, our membership program or our products, please visit us online at www.cnha.org or call (800) 840-8978.